WECULTURE

ENGAGE AND EMPOWER TEAMS TO DRIVE RESULTS

BY CHRIS CIULLA

DORRANCE
PUBLISHING CO
EST. 1920
PITTSBURGH, PENNSYLVANIA 15238

Dorrance Publishing Co
585 Alpha Drive
Pittsburgh, PA 15238
Visit our website at *www.dorrancebookstore.com*

ISBN: 978-1-4809-4691-0
eISBN: 978-1-4809-4714-6

FOREWORD
WE INCLUDES YOU

Great organizations are built through the collective efforts of great people. If you are the owner of a small business, this can be as simple as the first employee you hired who truly believed in your personal vision for a product or service. For large companies, government, civil servants, military, nonprofits, or religious groups, success comes from rallying toward a common goal. Why is this important?

How people behave and interact internally and externally will have lasting impact on the results of the enterprise. The secret is to have core values that act as a compass to guide behavior. This book will talk about what WeCulture is, why it is critical to driving results, how to leverage core values to create a great place to work, attracting the right talent, and a blueprint to build a forum that drives effort toward a common goal. That common goal could be revenue growth for companies, it could be to raise money to help those in need, or it could be a means to drive behavior to restore trust for government services or government leaders.

As you read on, think about your own organization and ask yourself how actively engaging your colleagues and leveraging common core values can impact the results of your organization.

Enjoy!

CONTENTS

WECULTURE

CORE VALUES TO GUIDE ACTION

SUCCESS THROUGH ENGAGEMENT AND EXECUTION

YOUR PART TO DRIVE WECULTURE

"The world as we have created it is a process of our thinking. It cannot be changed without changing our thinking."

— *Albert Einstein*

CHAPTER ONE
WHY WECULTURE?

Any great organization will only thrive with a well-defined culture, and in today's super-competitive market for the best talent, corporate culture takes center stage. What motivated employees twenty-five years ago has changed, and it will require how we lead to change with it. A recent Gallup Poll shows that across industries, only about one-third of employees in corporate America are actively engaged in their work; that means the other two-thirds are not. (Worldwide the same poll showed that number drops to only 13 percent of employees are actively engaged, and 87 percent are not). What is worse, there are those who are actively disengaged from the company who have a negative impact to results. Such a high level of disengaged employees collectively costs U.S. organizations between $450 to $550 billion. Why? Dissatisfied or disengaged employees don't give their best, and productive hours along with the spark of innovation are lost. Some truly disgruntled employees may actively work against the company goals and, in rare cases, put the enterprise at risk.

WeCulture is about engaging your employees by leveraging core values to grow the business. Core values are the cornerstone to govern behaviors and can be used as a means to actively engage colleagues. This common ground can motivate from leadership and also peer-to-peer. While many organizations have documented core values, my experience has been that leaders and staff alike could not name them. If you are not aware of what your organization's core values are, there is no hope that they can influence behavior. What is even more significant

1

is the new generation of talent and the value they place on corporate culture, even above compensation. Millennials are changing the workforce, and tactics used to motivate and retain top talent have changed, requiring a different approach. Technology has changed how we do business; our clients expect sales professionals to know more, offer more, deliver more. As the needs of our clients grow and become more complex, we need engaged people at all levels of the organization to win. Our colleagues need to be more sophisticated, requiring leaders to develop better hiring tactics, training, and retention strategies. Staff-level colleagues also play a critical role, and because today's workforce wants to be part of the greater good of the enterprise, we includes all staff, regardless of rank. WeCulture is not about leadership; it is about everyone's role in engaging employees to create a great culture. The idea is to build better internal relationships across all levels so that all employees look forward to coming to work each day. If this is achieved, retaining your best colleagues becomes easy. We not only want our place of work to be a great place to work — we also want common culture to be the cornerstone to drive financial results for all.

This book is not just for leaders; it is for anyone who wants to learn how to drive great corporate culture. I believe before I can share what WeCulture is, it might be important to know where it came from. Most people learn through failure; I am no different. Spending several years early on in my career focused on climbing the corporate ladder, there were many great lessons learned, skills acquired, and relationships that stand strong today. Before WeCulture can be shared and understood, I will offer a bit about me. This will outline some of my experiences that changed my career, life, and outlook on how to lead in any capacity. How I see life outside work has also changed for the better, and my relationship with my wife and two children has become stronger. My point of failure was an epiphany that spurred me to create WeCulture. At the time, it felt like my worst moment, but today I look back knowing it was the best thing that ever happened to me.

My father was a New York City firefighter, and my mother was primarily a stay-at-home mom. Once my brother and I hit middle school age, she went back to work as a part-time bookkeeper. I have two brothers: one is three years older and the other is my identical twin. Being a twin was an incredible experience. Before the age of cell phones, it was like having a comic book superpower, and we had plenty of fun. We looked so much alike, our own grandmother and friends from the neighborhood often would not immediately know that I was Chris. You can use your imagination to think for a moment on what kind of mischief you would get into if you had someone in your life who looked exactly like you living in New York City. I share this because part of who I am as an adult is born from this. Taking risks, my sense of humor, and the ability to stand out and be comfortable with it all come from a life standing next to a guy who looked exactly like me. Meeting new people was easy, plus add that we were both extroverts by nature. I learned how to build a network at a young age. It serves me well to this day.

We grew up on Staten Island. My first job was a paper route that I inherited from my older brother while in middle school. I made thirty dollars a week back then, which made me the richest kid in my class. This was the first brick in shaping my thoughts around the value of work — money=freedom. Before I had this job, if I wanted to go to a movie, buy clothing, or anything else, my parents would pay for it. Being in a working-class family, my parents were big on earning what you want, and I hated household chores...so having my own money was liberating. Aside from freedom, it built my confidence. If I wanted to go somewhere, I did not need a ride. I could get a cab or take a bus. My first date was a movie with a girl from school. I was in eighth grade. I grabbed a cab and went to her house to pick her up, hopped out, and knocked on the front door. Her dad answered and invited me in. I could tell by the look on his face there was concern.

"Is that your cab?" he asked.

I said yes, which prompted the next question in a pretty stern voice. "How old are you, kid?"

I explained we went to school together and were the same age, that I could take a cab because I had a job. I explained where we would go and when we would be back. Her dad did not smile when she came down to leave, but he said it was nice to meet me and reminded me to have her home on time. Freedom also gave me confidence.

High school was not that fun for me. I have no athletic ability — absolutely none. I played one season of football for a Pop Warner league and got the obligatory five plays a half. I loved football but was failing despite serious time and effort. So the time other kids put into sports, I put into work. I kept my paper route and got a job at McDonald's when I was a freshman. NYC required working papers under sixteen, and believe it or not, working there really made an impression on me. The owners took great pride in the business and their awards year after year as a top franchise for the organization. This was achieved through strict execution of the standard operating procedures, and the owner's son always shared results of corporate evaluations with every employee. He was a sharp leader and my first real boss, one of the hardest-working guys I ever met. Here I learned the value of process and how standard operating procedures can drive excellence. Our team knew the goals for the franchise and how each member must perform his or her role to make the team a success. Anyone on the team knew our goal for sales for a Saturday shift and what he or she had to do on his or her own station to win. Another lesson: rally your team by sharing organizational goals and results, and win or lose as a team.

There was a written procedure for every station: registers, grill, bun station, dressing table, and even to take out the trash and account for food/material waste. Every month your manager would come on the floor and work next to you to do an evaluation. At the end of your shift, there would be a thirty-minute meeting where you were rated on a scale of one to five on the station procedures, ability to display corporate values, and appearance, including required uniform. Because results were public, it was a competitive environment — high school kids flipping burgers and taking it seriously. That is the mark of good culture. Standard operating procedures consistently followed = results. Factor in teamwork, and five people following these procedures contributed to making every Big Mac. This was a big restaurant and super busy. On weekends there would be lines out the doors all day long from about 8:30 A.M. to 8 P.M., and we were open from 6 A.M. to 11 P.M. Through working there, I made several friends and was part of a winning business. It was hot as hell in the kitchen, but I loved going to work there and have many great memories.

I worked there for five years and kept this job while doing everything else I could do to make money. Because my dad owned rental properties, I hung Sheetrock, did demolition, and learned basic plumbing and electric with my twin brother. I even got a job with my math teacher who was a wedding photographer and did that two nights a weekend (sometimes after my 6 A.M. shift at McDonald's). As a wedding photographer's assistant, you really had to be great with people. My job was checking that all the equipment worked (before digital cameras, there was a ton of it) and making sure we got all the family together for group shots. If a bride was getting flustered in the park on a hot day taking pictures, I would get her a drink and hold a golf umbrella to keep her in the shade. Parents would pay big money for their kids to have huge weddings, and we made sure they had pictures for every moment of it, sometimes taking from four hundred to five hundred shots with professional film. I would work with them all day and get to know their extended family to ensure every person they loved was photographed. It was their day as a family, and we made every interaction about them. If you are a recent graduate reading this, you could never understand how much work it really was growing up without a cell phone and the technology to retouch pictures in the moment. Another lesson learned: customer first = repeat business. We would do events for the same families, and many people would request me personally.

My grades were about a 3.3, but my real education came through work, not class. In school I worked to get through the day and got grades to keep my parents happy. I did not have time to study from working all these jobs, so the fact that school came easy was a blessing.

I was pretty lazy about selecting a college, and at the time, there was less focus than there is today on selecting a school. My parents did not take me on some grand tour of the country to see dozens of universities. The choice was left to me, and because of the network I had, along with several jobs, I chose Baruch in Manhattan and remained home. College was better. I joined a club, the Italian American Society, and held office as VP. We had a budget, and I was able to apply the skills I learned working through high school. Socially I was pretty active, got good grades, and continued to work at least two jobs the whole way through. At nineteen I took a job as a waiter for a catering hall and was promoted to waiter captain. I made one hundred to two hundred dollars per night on average, including tips. I wore a full tuxedo and got to apply my love of working with people with the lesson of following procedures to make every event great for our guests. Because of McDonald's, I already understood structure made the job easy to do, and looking sharp brought a level of respect from staff and the guests — pressed tuxedo, shined shoes, and starched shirt for every shift. I got to apply the lessons learned from two previous jobs here that helped me excel. Another reason I loved this job was because I met my wife working there. We are married over twenty happy years with two children. Another lesson: learned skills are transferable from job to job and can give you an edge in a competitive environment.

I graduated college in in the early nineties in the middle of a recession, getting a job in an inbound customer service center for a shipping line. Truthfully I took this job because it was what I could get at the time. I was bored out of my mind and worked for someone who absolutely hated the company. It was a Korean-owned carrier, and the executives who were ex-pats thought Americans were lazy at best. The only good that came of it was that it led to my first sales job only three months later for another transportation company. Selling was great. I was an extrovert who values repeatable processes to drive results. Combined that with several years of working with people, and I quickly became a top-ranking player on the team. I was assigned key clients within the first year on the job because of new accounts I was able to bring in. Selling in this industry was seasonal. We had a big push in Q1 and Q2 to get contracts signed for the year and then spent the other two quarters servicing existing clients. I made lots of calls overseas to ensure cargo made ships through the summer and fall. Servicing existing clients also included lots of golf, lunches, dinners, parties, and late nights out. Most clients signed in the first half of the year would be over seven figures in revenue; a few were larger and mid-eight-figure clients. Here selling was an individual effort for each account manager. I was responsible for the inbound trade from Asia to the U.S., and the clients I sold to imported electronic goods, toys, and artificial Christmas decorations. I did this for five years until, by chance, I fell into staffing and have been in the industry ever since.

My first three years in staffing was with an international firm. This company had 119 offices in the U.S., Australia, and Europe. Staffing was completely different from my last job; the sale was completely transactional in nature. The average sales per transaction was about twelve thousand to fifteen thousand dollars, and a large client would be low- to mid-six figures, creating a never-ending need for new clients. The year had peaks and valleys for demand, but consistent activity could drive results. The focus on new business was year-round, and we serviced clients in the moment. Selling here was through teamwork, partnering with recruiters who sourced candidates.

I was rookie of the year, setting a record for gross-profit dollars that stood several years after. I was quickly promoted to sales manager for the office. By year two, I was a top-ten individual contributor worldwide while leading a sales team. I loved the job and the people I worked with; my boss was a pretty stern guy but always had my back. We hired several people together, and my first hire was a rookie of the year as well and runs that office to this day. While I was sales manager, we took the office from #28 to #3. I was partnered with a great recruiting manager, and she played a big part in our success. Lessons of consistency and teamwork applied that I learned early on again provided an edge to win. My ambition drove me to leave, and that leads us to the beginning of my failure that helped me create WeCulture.

I was recruited by a publicly traded company with over three hundred offices and seven divisions to be a branch manager over two teams. My motivation was wrong from the start. I took the job for a promotion opportunity first and considered the company values as a distant second. This was my first management role leading people through other managers. I'm a history buff, and in my mind, this company was the Roman Empire — growth through aggressive expansion and crush the competition was the market strategy. As I was trained, my peers and leaders taught me how to systematically find the competitions' clients and make them ours. Their values were tied to financial growth, and your report card as a leader was your profit and loss statement. While this is all good business strategy, I learned something else about their values: People were a means to an end. We hired aggressively and fired quickly. After six months of being there, my understanding was that this company was 99 percent their way and 1 percent original thinking. My boss was a regional vice president and by far the smartest guy I have ever met. He started as a sales person working a desk and ran one of the most successful regions for the company when I joined. We were the same age, and he seemed like a guy who could take over the world. My office was in a small market, and I was surrounded by other branch managers who had been with the company for years. I guess he saw something in me because he invested his time mentoring me in the first year, focusing on how to hire, evaluate talent, and drive the business. I learned how to read a financial statement, leverage Key Performance Indicator reporting to measure effort, and that success breeds opportunity. My first year, that small office grew through a recession, and I was promoted to a larger office, which was the heart of the region. There were several veteran producers here, and hiring internal staff was a full-time job; for the first time in my career, my success was not tied to personal production.

This is where I got lost. I was encouraged to shake off the blue-collar guy; the gritty, hardworking, slightly overweight, Italian guy from Staten Island who helped me as a personal producer had no use in my new role for this company. My boss introduced me to several key executives who told me how to dress, speak, interact with my peers, and present in public. Within a few months, I was wearing suspenders, pin-striped suits, and wing-tip shoes, and it only got worse. In a small office, I was on my own and saw my peers at quarterly meetings, but here I interacted with them almost daily. Many of the divisions I was charged to lead provided services to satellite markets. We were encouraged to compete internally. Divisions were set up with "overlap," meaning we actually would be competing within the organization. This competition created lots of conflict and internal drama. At the time, I thought it was crazy — just like wearing suspenders — but I figured, this is how it is done to climb the ladder, so I aggressively ran my office to grow, even if I had to push the limits with my peers in the organization. Most interactions internally were focused purely on first-order consequences and that was how leaders were encouraged to make decisions. When debating through a tough decision, I would be asked by my boss, "What would you do if our COO was asking? How would it look, Chris, that you are unsure?" Second- and third-order consequences were an afterthought, almost like damage control as needed. Core values were trumped by how things looked to your audience in the moment. My inflated ego took center stage and drove me even deeper into the horrible person I had become.

Two years later I was promoted to a regional-vice-president role in another part of the country. By now I was completely institutionalized to the culture of this company. My inner core values were lost behind the cardboard-cutout leader I had become. I had a reputation for being good at hiring and even better at weeding out underperformers. My peers from the region I left were happy to see me go because it created opportunity, and my overinflated ego went with me. My new boss was a district president. When I met her, I thought she was sharp. In appearance she was a female version of my old boss, but her style was to the far negative extreme of the culture. People represented no value and were a means to an end; she was quite clear on this in the interview process. If my old boss's region was Rome, my new leader was running ancient Egypt. (We would build the business even if it meant crushing the staff under the stones of our success.) My own arrogance blinded me to all the warning signs of who she was because I figured I would always add value through growth. She was super sharp, and while very cold, she taught me about budgeting and forecasting. I quickly mastered the skill and could produce my own budget annually for six offices that had over twenty divisions. Together over three years, we grew the business from $29 million to $57 million in my region, opened new divisions, and had the highest net-income percentage in the company. I was paid well and paraded around at meetings like a prized pet. By now my ego was an eight-hundred-pound gorilla and out of control. In public my success brought high praise, and the team I was charged to lead seemed happy to follow. What I did not realize was that my troops hated me. I hired and fired more people than I can count, and being in smaller markets in the Southeast, this killed my personal reputation. I was completely blind to this, or worse, thought it would never catch up with me.

During this "ego trip," my wife carried more than her fair share of the load at home in a new city. I missed almost every school event for my kids, who were both in grade school. I worked from 7:30 A.M. to 6:30 P.M. every day, not including commuting an hour each way. I traveled Tuesdays through Thursdays and took my BlackBerry on vacations. I rarely took time off and never disengaged from the office — I cannot believe my wife pushed through without complaint. She should have taken the kids and left me. I was a horrible father and barely a good husband. My relationship with our children suffered; the lost time and memories are something I regret to this day.

When the real-estate crash came, things really came undone. The business took a big hit; we were firing people almost every Friday. Offices with sixty people shrank to about fifteen, and leaders on the team were demoted or released. One morning I got ready for work and realized my staff weren't the only people who hated me. I hated the person I had become and despised the fact that I abandoned my own core values. At the end of this road, I lost the opportunity to lead and left the company in disgrace. I was stunned and needed time to reflect on how this could possibly happen after so many years of financial success.

I had eight weeks before I started a new job with another company. It was then that I decided to make a list of all the things I had learned in the 8½ years I was with the firm so I could interview effectively. While I made the list, I also read a book — *True North* by Bill George — and there I realized the need to define my own core values and find a company where they fit. Through this book and self-reflection, the point of failure was clear: I had abandoned who I was to be what the company wanted and failed because it conflicted with my own values. Without core values to guide my actions, my ego easily set in and turned me into a management monster. I was the type of boss you would see in a bad movie. Smart people who worked for me eventually saw right through me and either quit or just tolerated me as a bad leader. I took time to reconnect with my own values and created a list of things that would define team culture if I was fortunate enough to lead again.

Virtues based on "we," not "I," the greater good of the people I was charged to lead, and focusing on long-term outcomes to help all colleagues make more money than last year. All were rooted in three basic core values: Pedal the Bike, Be Positive, and Honesty/Ethics First...WeCulture.

A few years later I landed my first opportunity to put WeCulture to use driving a failed business to success, placing these three core values as our compass to guide actions to positive financial results. This book will talk about the journey and how a determined team can leverage cultural change to drive results. With a new generation entering the workforce (Millennials), how organizations led the Baby Boomers and Generation X will need to change. WeCulture is designed to focus on this ever-growing segment of our workforce while leveraging core values to engage everyone on the team, regardless of age, title, or personal disposition. Let's be clear. The goal of any business is to make money. WeCulture is not about some touchy-feely, everyone-gets-a-trophy environment. This is about having an actively engaged workforce. It is about creating the forum for all colleagues to perform at their best while working within groups to make their team the best — all while getting better financial results for themselves and the company. Success for the company breeds opportunity for all, and being part of a winning team is the best way to retain top talent.

For a mid-sized company, it takes four actively engaged colleagues to balance out the negative impact of a disengaged employee. For large companies, the ratio is ten actively engaged employees to one disengaged employee. Why? Disengaged colleagues deliver less work product and lower quality. Their interactions, internally and externally to the organization, at best are just going through the paces. Service to hard-won clients suffers, and your best colleagues have to pick up the slack. Left unchecked, disengaged colleagues will spread their behavior to others in the organization. Some colleagues will remain engaged and soldier on; others will join the disengagement train, and your best and brightest will eventually quit. This turnover will impact the hard costs of rehiring and training — and lost clients. Think about your current team. If you were honest, what is your ratio of engaged versus disengaged colleagues? What is the cost to your company and colleagues? How are you managing your own behavior to keep everyone actively engaged to drive results?

Embracing culture change is never easy and will expose weaknesses in the business that may need to be addressed. As you decide if WeCulture is right for your organization, don't let fear of change govern your actions. Don't let the negative thoughts centered around specific individuals stop you. If your company has a large leadership team, you will need their commitment. Core values have no meaning if they do not govern behavior to drive results. WeCulture keeps things simple, with each core value designed to support the other while unifying teams to the common goal of every business: making money. Chapter Two Brings us to the first question we need to answer before WeCulture can take hold: Who creates the culture?

"It is not in the stars to hold our destiny but in ourselves."
— *William Shakespeare*

CHAPTER TWO

WHO CREATES THE CULTURE?

Many companies have written core values and boast of having a great culture. As I look at posts on Facebook pages and LinkedIn, there are photos of softball games, charity events, and other various team-building exercises. All of these things are fun and get colleagues together outside the office, but these are "symptoms" of good culture, a by-product of what truly unifies a team. Hiring the right people is only part of the path to success. Companies go to great expense to find the best talent, but if people don't work together toward a common goal, turnover will follow. Great people cannot create great culture without simple core values to govern actions that are followed by all. Can well-defined, simple core values help turn around a failing business? How can core values be used to change culture for the better? More importantly, who creates the culture?

My new role was managing director for an international professional-services firm. I was called for this job by a recruiter I have known for years; I consider her a close friend to this day. My current role was great, and I took the meeting as a chance to network a bit. My friend who referred me suggested the idea, and I shared with her that I was not looking for a job. Her closing thoughts when I finally agreed to go to the meeting were, "Hey Chris, open your mind and have a long talk with yourself on the train ride uptown." She was right; I liked my current job, but I was still executing someone else's vision. WeCulture was still on the sidelines — an idea that had not seen practical application. Her advice was sound, and I spent most of the train ride up telling myself to listen.

It was a great French restaurant in midtown where I met my new boss, who was a seventeen-year veteran with the firm. We had some basic small talk and had lots of things in common — both married with kids about the same age. Like me, he grew up from a sales desk in our business and found himself leading a sixty-million-dollar region with six offices. He is someone very easy to like — professional, warm, friendly, and most importantly, a great communicator. As the conversation got down to business, we went through the normal interview paces as he asked about skills and accomplishments. I was honest with him about my eight years with a competitor and the basic lessons I learned from it. This is when we started to really dig in to the situation for one of the markets he was charged to lead.

The opportunity was opened due to the last leader being let go for failure to perform. I asked questions about what those causes were and could not believe a business under a seasoned veteran could reach such a low point. The office was performing so poorly that the global CEO and CFO for a twenty-five-billion-dollar parent company flew in from Europe for a two-day visit. For executives at this level to take action like this is almost unprecedented, and they spent time with all colleagues in the office to find the reason why this office was trending down in a growing economy. He shared the story of the visit in detail. The former MD was a sales person promoted to the role. About one year in, top-line revenue for the business was down significantly year over year, and the office had serious turnover. These visiting executives were people I would meet later on after taking the job, and they could smell BS a mile out. My new boss sat in all the meetings horrified, watching as his MD and staff were questioned. He admitted he let things go way too long. At the end of the meetings, he rode to the airport with these leaders, and parting thoughts were that they would be watching closely and to get this business back on track. That was two months before our dinner. Over coffee I asked questions about corporate culture and leadership style. This company had been acquired by the parent company only two years earlier, and the answers when I asked about core values were vague at best. As I continued to probe, his final answer was, "Our company is very entrepreneurial; local leaders can do what is needed to win."

This was the opportunity: a failed business with a new boss that was really hands-off and had no real focus on corporate culture. I went home thinking about the situation and the job with a nervous excitement. A rebuild like this was all hard work, hiring new staff, lots of personal selling, and long hours. The reputation of this office inside the company was mud. This opportunity had some other red flags. It would be the smallest business in revenue and direct reports I would be charged to lead for ten years, the pay was a lateral move, and the RVP had no clear vision beyond year one. The real question I kept coming back to was, can this be the chance to put WeCulture to practice? I interviewed with two more executives, and the answer quickly turned to yes. Even senior leaders could not tell me their own core values or define their culture consistently; it was as if they worked for different companies. There was no standard already set, and being left alone in a field office with no interference from a micromanaging VP could let me put WeCulture to the test.

I started three weeks later on a Wednesday. On my first day, my boss flew in to escort me to the office. We had breakfast at the hotel, and he reminded me that this job would be no picnic. I promised him that the first three to four weeks would be all observation and help to close deals as needed. When we walked in, there were nine people — eight staff plus the office manager. No one even got up to greet us. As we went desk to desk for introductions, we received brief handshakes — no smiles or small talk. The office was dirty, paint was scuffed waist-high on the walls, the chairs were stained, and some were at least fifteen to twenty years old. The carpets were worn, and boxes and papers were everywhere. There were sixteen cubicles; the empty ones had old computer equipment piled in them with a layer of dust. Then I noticed something really telling: The staff of eight producers were spaced in the sixteen cubicles, sitting as far apart as possible. No one was on the phones, and no one talked to each other; it was clear there was lots of conflict. I thought the silence might be for my benefit. My new office was not cleaned up from my predecessor. All his personal effects were still there, and the main floor looked neat compared to the place I would sit. I looked at my boss and said, "I would like to sit on the floor with the team for a few days, get a feel for how things work." Truthfully it was easier to clean a desk in my suit than that office. (I stayed late that Friday and cleaned it out, going through files. It took about five hours...at least it was clean.)

On day two, my boss hosted a staff meeting in the conference room, and I got the chance to see the team interact. As they talked through the sales opportunities, I watched the delivery team take notes but ask few questions. The ones they did ask got canned answers and short responses from the sales team. As the meeting ended, there was no recap to prioritize or assign workload. It was clear that the sales team had few real deals to close. I stayed behind with my new leader and reviewed production by colleague, and with the exception of one sales professional who had a large client, everyone else was below the company performance standard. As we looked at KPI's, I could see why — phone call and client meeting numbers were the lowest in the company. After that my new leader packed to leave and dropped this little heads-up. "By the way, our division CEO will be here in the first ninety days to check on progress. You should have a business plan ready for the visit, and I'll put it on your calendar. I'll check in a couple of weeks to see how things are going. Good luck."

Friday I observed and took notes. Not much to see — the day came and went. Over the weekend, I sent out calendar invites for staff one-on-one meetings. Observe for a couple of weeks to soak things in? I had seen enough in three days. With the CEO coming to town, it would take every minute we had to get this team ready — no reason to put off the path to change. Doing the same things the same way would only yield the same results.

To prepare for one-on-one meetings, I made sure everyone would be asked the same questions about culture. One at time they came in, and it went something like this.

"So what are some of the challenges you feel we have with the business?" This would be my first business question after about thirty minutes of very positive small talk.

When I got to one of the salespeople, a four-year colleague, the answer was, "The culture at this company sucks."

"What is so terrible about the company culture?" I asked.

"This place is so negative; everyone is out for themselves...there is no teamwork here."

"Let me ask a question. The company has core values. Do you know what they are?"

"Well no, but why does it matter? Whatever they are, no one follows them."

"So how does corporate influence our culture here?"

"I guess they don't."

Now we were getting somewhere. I kept asking questions.

"How often does our RVP or other members of the leadership team visit the office?"

"Other than those guys from Europe who fired my old boss and introducing you...almost never."

"So if we are in a field office largely left alone out here, then who creates the culture?"

As soon as I asked, there was silence and then the response. "You do. You are the leader, and leaders are supposed to drive culture."

"I agree, but I know who I bring to work every day. I'm a guy who brushes his teeth in the morning, thinking how today will be one little bit better than yesterday for all of us. Who do you bring to work every day? Is it someone who thinks it sucks here or someone who will work with me to make it better?"

Silence again. "I'm ready to commit to make it better if you are," she said.

"I'm glad to hear it because we can use all the help we can get."

And there it was. We established common ground. I was able to get this person to understand that the company does not create the culture. The company might define the desired core values, but it cannot drive execution alone. It is the leader who sets the tone, and together with colleagues, we all create the culture. We talked a bit longer, and I shared with her the three core values to gain commitment.

> Pedal the Bike
> Be Positive
> Honest and Ethical

This became the foundation of all the one-on-one meetings, and I asked each colleague to make the same commitment, promising they could hold me accountable, and I would hold them accountable anytime we did not display these values in our daily work. Later in the week, we met as a team and committed to our core values, writing them on the whiteboard. This would be the beginning of change for the better, a defining part of what WeCulture is. Getting the team to come to the realization that we all create the culture takes away the excuse that someone else is driving bad culture. If accountability for culture transcends titles or rank, this can be empowering for everyone on the team. People want to be a part of something and will tolerate a challenging environment if they can be an agent of change. We will go deeper into each core value later on.

In the staffing business, we interview candidates every day. People leave companies because of their boss and reasons that always boil down to poor or lacking corporate culture. It is very rare candidates tell me the main reason for leaving a job is pay. There will always be a better paycheck somewhere, but a small raise is usually a short-term fix for job satisfaction in the wrong company. The reason culture fails in an organization is because of one critical element: It must be "followed by all." Working with companies large and small, I find that leaders even on the same team share with candidates during panel interviews conflicting values on how to drive success at their company. The manager talks about hard work, and then in the final interview, some VP drones on about positioning yourself on the most visible projects to mix with the right people. Conflicting core values creates conflict between colleagues, backdoor politics, or worse — avoidance. If your employees don't work together and communicate well (and often), even the smallest short-term, common-sense goal becomes unattainable. Conflicting internal politics creates opposing subgroups that can disrupt productivity. Often leaders have to break up sparring matches and pick a winning idea. Losing team members in the subgroup actively work to sink the project. The easy tool is avoidance, making themselves unavailable to complete the mission, and everyone loses.

How can this be solved? Where do we start? If your company has published core values, put it to the first test. Ask leaders who report to you if they can tell you the core values in your next one-on-one. If they cannot, then there is no possible way the company's vision for culture will govern actions at any level. By the way, this is not their fault. There is only one person you can hold accountable for this, and it requires an introspective look. As a leader, you are responsible to be the keeper of core values for your team, to make them known, to display them in your actions, and to have them followed by all. Every level of leadership, every middle manager, and every colleague should know the core values of the company and display those core values in every action they take. Let's take a lesson from this and start now. If you are a leader at a company, call Human Resources and get a copy of the organization's core values. If you are an owner and do not have written core values, we can talk more about leveraging the WeCulture leadership tool kit to partner with your team to create them. Once you have core values defined, meet with your direct reports and review each core value, giving them life and meaning through practical discussion on how they apply to your business. If your team has direct reports, they should have the same meeting with their team with you attending to help facilitate for consistency of the message. This is the foundation of every action taken and should not be left to filter down. Be an active participant in the rollout down to the staff level. Your colleagues will appreciate the time and attention, and if you routinely manage via chain of command, this will give you valuable time with staff. Once this is done, post the core values everywhere and hold each other accountable to them.

For me, WeCulture is a corporate moral compass, setting a standard that promotes teamwork. Pedal the Bike is a commitment to drive personal activity. Be Positive focuses action on how we can do things better and not why we can't. Honest and Ethical means we tell the truth no matter what. If it costs us a sale, so be it. If you make a mistake, tell the team, and we will fix it together. I challenge every colleague, regardless of their position, to hold me and other employees to it. If everyone is governed by the same values and truly holds each other accountable, corporate politics wither away, and partnership toward our quantifiable goals takes center stage. No more conflicting subgroups lobbying for resources after meetings — anyone can speak up in a meeting to share ideas. Challenging the status quo becomes a means of continuous improvement. WeCulture creates the forum where this can happen, and with obstacles out of the way, real work gets done. This is how culture can drive results. Common core values, when followed, foster teamwork; combine teamwork with transparency around our quantifiable goals, and success will follow. Something to consider: Successful teams retain talent — good culture is now a retention tool. People stay with companies when they like their team and feel productive in their jobs.

Now where was I? Right...two weeks in to a new job, and we just established our core values for the team, agreeing to hold each other to them. So what do we do when one of our core values is ignored by a teammate or direct report? I got my first real test in week three with a recruiter. I promised myself that I would give every person a clean slate no matter what was said in our one-on-one meetings. Her meeting with me was focused on everything her colleagues were doing that prevented her own success — all blame and no personal accountability for her own actions. She was pretty direct and suggested change here would be impossible. "You have a great vision, Chris. I hope you can do it for both of us." The meeting was the worst of the group, and her negative energy was over the top. I accepted her thoughts and politely ended the meeting, letting her know she would be held to our three core values.

Although most leaders would have pushed this colleague hard, you cannot invite honest feedback and use it against someone. This is an easy way to violate trust. She had very low KPI's, the lowest financial results versus goal on the delivery team. Her go-to response was always some form of "We can't," "Okay, I guess we can try," or "We have done that already." I decided to put her to the test and gave her our best client job order to work on right in the sweet spot of her network. The best way to see if someone will Pedal the Bike is to give them something they are capable of doing without a hint of doubt. After our job-order meeting, I was leaving for a client visit and heard her outside having a cigarette with another colleague, complaining about her assignment and how the sales team would never sell the candidates she found through her hard work. She did not see me as I walked past because her back was facing me. Most leaders would make a note and move on, but we had agreed to hold each other accountable. When I came back from the client meeting, I invited her to the office and told her what I had heard. After a bit of defense from her, I let her know that any negative energy was against our core values. If anyone has constructive feedback on how we can do better, we can all listen and work toward change as a team. Most of her defense was to call the sales team lazy, incompetent, and people who just didn't deserve her work. Personal attacks are a type of feedback that is culture cancer: complaining. Culture cancer is a term we use to describe behavior that can put the team or enterprise goals at risk. Culture cancer, when ignored, can spread to other colleagues or teams. Taken a step further, it can govern actions in a negative way, having adverse effects on the organization. Think about the example above with this recruiter. If colleagues had heard her description of their performance, how could teamwork be possible? When this happens, ask what specific actions can be taken to improve the situation.

After looking in vain for some constructive feedback that we could act on together, I ended the meeting by sharing that I was disappointed that she had broken her commitment to Be Positive. In order for culture to take hold, leaders cannot tolerate lack of adoption of core values. I'm pretty strict and hold myself to a firm, three-strikes-rule maximum. Before the end of the same week, she hit the nerve two more times, and in a meeting, another member of delivery called her out, asking her to stop being so negative. On the third instance, she went an entire day without any documented activity on the assignment given to her (the job right in her network). Negative and not Pedaling the Bike. I invited her in the office and immediately let her go. I remember the look of shock on her face, but

I told her, today was her last day because she failed to adopt the core values we had agreed to only a few days earlier. This was while the rest of the team was honoring their commitment — three days of activity above the metrics, lots of positive talk to overcome challenges, and an honest approach to their work. After she packed her desk, I asked the team into the conference room and let them know today was this colleague's last day. I was completely transparent on the reason why, and our twenty-five-year veteran replied, "It is about time. Her attitude was killing us."

At the end of the day, I called my RVP to share the news. He was surprised I had let her go.

"Chris, can we really afford to lose such an experienced recruiter? I'm concerned. I mean, what will our CEO say?"

All the wrong questions. What people think of you when you act is a first-order consequence. If you are truly committed to driving culture, sometimes it will take hard choices. I knew he would not be happy and that my decision would create a bit of doubt in the moment, but I was focused on second- and third-order consequences of my actions. Letting her go was hard today but showed my commitment to our core values. This is absolutely critical to the long-term success of driving culture.

Keeping this experienced colleague might help me in the very near term, but not holding her accountable would tell the rest of the team we were not serious about the cultural change we discussed. Back to the conversation with our salesperson ("I'm ready to commit to make it better if you are.") Once you show you are not committed, you lose the commitment from the rest of the team. By the way, this salesperson from that first conversation became our top producer. Any lack of resolve says to the team the commitment to culture is lip service, a lie, a reason to look for a new job. Here is a lesson I have learned managing people since 1997. Bad employees = bad things; the longer you keep bad employees around, the better chance that bad things happen to you and the team. Keep bad people, and your high-potential colleagues who every competitor wants will leave. Why? No one wants to be on a losing team with bad culture. No talented person wants to pedal the bike harder because of another colleague not putting in 100 percent. People who follow the virtue of Be Positive don't want to work with negative energy. Honest and ethical people check out immediately if they believe their company promotes, or even tolerates, immoral behavior. Once your best people leave, all that is left is your culture-cancer colleagues. Best you get rid of the wrong people quickly to give the right people the opportunity to drive culture with you.

Over the next month, we had record activity for five weeks in a row. The team had steam in their stride, and there was that buzz of activity that just feels good: people on the phones, talking to each other, some high fives, and deals being booked. Three simple core values governing actions helped us turn things in the right direction in a matter of weeks — just in time. In a few weeks, our CEO would be in town with my RVP to check on progress.

We were teed up for a great visit, and this was my first time meeting the CEO. After almost a year of only two to three transactions a month, twelve weeks into my taking the job, we had ten consultants going to work and nine more booked for next month. We opened the day with a daily "board-meeting" review and opened orders and assignments. We set up a new job-order board to track KPI's and transactions through the sales process. I moved it to the main bullpen from the conference room, keeping our activity on public display. My RVP smiled as we went through the meeting. The team spoke with confidence; there was a bit of laughing and joking, which is healthy for a sales team. I had a presentation planned for our CEO to review progress, and when I was invited to the conference room, I asked the team to join me. If I was going to share the results of our hard work, they should be present for the moment, especially since they had a ringside seat for the last disaster visit in February from our parent company. Our success was a team effort created through commitment to our core values.

We started with a great run, and by the end of the year, the business had grown in head count by 50 percent, and the next year's top-line revenue grew another 45 percent. We made several hires and outgrew the office space. By year three, we were in a new space, the staff was twenty-five strong, we retained five of the original nine colleagues, and we won Circle of Excellence awards as a business two years in a row. This office was now a top-ranked market for the company, built on the foundation of the same people who were so unsuccessful. What created the change? It was adoption of core values by the team, a culture that held each other accountable to Pedal the Bike, Be Positive, and Honest and Ethical. WeCulture — it was fostering the idea that every colleague creates the culture through their own actions, and a healthy culture yields great financial results. As time went on, I had a saying to keep people accountable to our core values in a positive way. If there was a tough moment, we reminded each other, "We includes you."

Who creates the culture? "We" do. Define your core values, communicate them down to the frontline of your organization, and hold the team accountable to them without exception. As my responsibilities for this company grew, WeCulture expanded beyond my home market. We had Fatheads made for the walls displaying core values and the virtues to drive behavior. We had giveaway items to share with colleagues that displayed our core values — bracelets, lapel pins, polo shirts, and all kinds of other items. Sounds easy, right? Let's dig deeper into how each core value works and how leaders can use them to drive behavior.

"Define what your brand stands for, its core values and tone of voice, then communicate consistently in those terms"

Simon Mainwaring

CORE VALUES
TO GUIDE ACTION

"Individual commitment to a group effort — that is what makes a team work, a company work, a society work, a civilization work"

— *Vince Lombardi*

CHAPTER THREE
PEDAL THE BIKE

Many organizations across industries have key performance indicators (KPI's) to measure the effectiveness of the business. The definition of KPI's from Wikipedia.org: *A performance indicator or key performance indicator (KPI) is a type of performance measurement. KPIs evaluate the success of an organization or of a particular activity in which it engages.* Almost all organizations use KPI's to measure performance, bringing the quantitative measurement down to the staff level and evaluating individual contribution to the business. Manufacturing will track units produced, rework time, staff overtime, downtime for equipment, inventory, levels, material waste, etc. Customer service outsourcing will track calls taken, received, average hold times, call success rates, and satisfaction survey results. Name an industry or business, and they have KPI's to measure performance.

KPI's can be used as a positive reinforcement and rally point for the team. WeCulture can help organizations focus on creating KPI's that help them win by measuring how colleagues contribute to team goals. To understand how this works, first we have to understand where KPI's can go wrong and undermine desired behaviors. As you read on, think about your company and how KPI's are currently used. Sure, they are an accountability tool, but how much of what we track and count is actually driving revenue growth? How does the data we track help teams succeed and achieve their goals? How does each colleague view KPI's?

Is there a connection on how individual effort impacts the team? Does how an employee views KPI impact just how seriously they apply effort?

I'm a born-bred, bonus-fed salesperson. My entire career was selling as a top performer and then leading sales teams. Let's use this domain as a point of focus and see what we can take away from it. In sales, KPI's are often used to measure effort. Organizations will track everything from dials, "talk time," connecting phone calls, client visits/presentations, order activity, close ratios, cycle times... the list goes on. By the time all of these metrics come out to the managers, it is a history lesson. The individuals they are charged to lead will have so much information that it becomes hard to know what is important. If you think managers are confused by data overload, sit with the sales teams and ask them what they think of KPI's. Senior leaders often focus on the KPI's that worked when they were salespeople; some executives in large companies never sold at all. I had five different managers in four years at the company where I launched WeCulture. The COO twice and he had never sold anything in his career. He was an accountant from the Big Four and transferred from a CFO role to COO. Of all the leaders, I felt he understood KPI's more than the others who grew up from the sale ranks. Something salespeople hear all the time from senior leaders who have not worked a desk in several years — which makes them instantly tune out — "Back when I was selling, we used to..." In the years that have passed by, technology has evolved new means of reaching target audiences, diminishing the value of old methods. Here is an example: Pushing dials for connects has changed dramatically due to technology since I have started selling. In the 1990s, caller ID for business was a new and not widely used technology. The return on outbound dials to connects was about five to ten dials to one connect depending on your market and target audience. Today I sit with salespeople making calls, and we can make one hundred dials in a day and get three to five connecting calls. When this happens, KPI's often become a negative to colleagues, and even to frontline managers. The more we push for individual activity, the less we get. Even worse, smart sales professionals will learn to work to a KPI and game the system. This is another form of culture cancer that can doom a business to failure — salespeople focusing on activity for a pat on the head above activity to generate sales.

Case in point: Remember that company I shared earlier where I spent over eight years? They measured weekly billable hours for consultants on assignment per individual contributor, client visits, and connecting phone calls. There were several others, but these were the primary published results ticked on every job-order board in every bullpen. So what is important to the growth of the business and successful financial results? As the leader, the choice was easy: billable hours. That is what generates revenue, gross profit, and net income. We would celebrate growth in billable hours and hold contests and events on a regular basis. All were very positive ways to reinforce that this was what we wanted; all other KPI's we measured were a means to an end. So where did it go sideways? We had colleagues on the team for years that were President's Club winners based on billed hours. Every producer was responsible for 125 connecting phone calls and ten client meetings a week. If one of these top billers missed 125 connects and ten meetings more than two weeks in a row, we would call them to the office for a detailed activity review and demand 125 and ten. Frontline leaders were trained to do this without question, and at the time, I was one of them. Some top performers would consistently miss on connects or visits and brave the thirty minutes in the office every Monday. Others would game the system and put false activity in the database to keep their bosses away. This was known throughout the organization and was a morale killer. One of the best sales professionals I ever worked with (top-ten producer worldwide for his division) would end every team meeting with "Glad we wrapped this up; I have 125 connects to make." Then he would roll his eyes and go. We spent so much time focusing on KPI's, we were eroding our own culture even for the people who gave us the best results. Colleagues gaming the system would spend a few hours a week doing it, and that meant less time on meaningful selling. We treated every colleague exactly the same. As we focus on individuals and his or her personal performance, we take the focus off the team. Bad culture = employee turnover. As an organization, this company had some of the highest turnover in the industry and was the subject of ridicule on social-media outlets. All the bad press just made it harder to attract talent and made the job of a frontline manager even harder. WeCulture is about what matters and puts focus on efforts that yield results. The colleagues Pedal the Bike. How can we avoid KPI's eroding culture? How can we leverage KPI's to create positive energy and good culture to drive results?

DRIVE METRICS THAT MATTER

The market has changed, so the KPI's measured a decade ago will likely not add the same level of value for the organization. If these metrics fail in achieving the company goals, they are sure to fail the individual contributors we are charged to lead. In the example above, all the focus on connect calls worked well for this company in the 1990s, but as technology brought us VOIP, smartphones, and social media, sales professionals have an arsenal of tools at their disposal to make first contact with a prospect that goes well beyond a phone call. In our industry, client visits, job orders, submittals, and placements are the measure of how we impact financial results to drive individual and company success. If these KPI's are the measure to yield mutually assured value, why count calls? Why should managers focus so closely on how we get to the activities that matter? If we focus on getting a client meeting, then WeCulture encourages leaders to focus on KPI's that drive mutually assured value for the company and the colleague.

In the example above of counting calls, we did not care if a colleague got us the mutual value of exceeding billable hours. We still pushed connects just because it was below our corporate, slide-rule standard. For our tenured high performers, KPI's to drive results are different. This population needed to make fewer calls and spend more time on visits maximizing opportunity at active clients. Sure they need new logos too, but not as much as a new hire with no active clients. New hires work really hard on first-contact activity that includes every tool available and go beyond the outbound dial, build to visits, job orders, interviews, and close deals. After we have enough companies signed, shift KPI focus more on client-facing activity. Millennials bring new skills. They are experts on social-media communication and grew up using these tools hundreds of times each day. If this is their means to get meetings to hit the client-visit KPI, then we achieve the KPI that matters. As we focus on nurturing a skill the colleague has to leverage the KPI's we need to win, there is no need for colleagues to focus on driving activity that has low yield. Better yet, no need to game the system by fluffing out dated methods. Time is spent selling, not eroding culture.

MAKE METRICS ABOUT "WE"

A team approach to KPI's can help avoid the pitfalls created through individual focus and unify the group toward the common goal to grow revenue. Right now you are reading and saying to yourself, selling is about individual contribution...

what is the team approach? Why focus on team first and individual second? The answer is Millennials. According to the Social Security Administration, Baby Boomers are aging out at the rate of about ten thousand per day, which means Millennials are becoming a much larger population in the workforce. This generation of workers has different drivers. Money is a means to live, and career is about being part of something that is a force for good. They don't want a job. Millennials want to contribute to the greater goal and understand how what they do every day drives success for the team. Routine, repetitive tasks done alone can be kryptonite to even the most motivated new hire. If you want this generation to really engage, then the culture must focus on the greater good and a team approach.

Plug in KPI's, and WeCulture teaches leaders how to drive desired behavior by creating team goals — everyone Pedals the Bike. If being part of the greater good is a main behavioral driver for the colleague, then why spend time focused on individual contribution? Keep in mind we are not saying we don't track individual stats. What WeCulture does is report the KPI's as a team KPI and then outlines how each team member contributed to the goal. The team succeeds or fails as a unit, with everyone's activity posted for all to see. WeCulture takes it one step further and highlights those who exceeded the goal and will even comment on how this helped the team get a specific win. These stories share how the individual benefitted, yet the primary focus is on how that win was a cornerstone for the team win. Managers who practice this approach still do one-on-ones with each employee. What we found is that when the team is put first, each member will focus on pulling their weight through meeting or exceeding KPI's.

Back to what WeCulture is; everyone creates the culture and holds each other accountable at a peer level. If the team goals come first, no colleague who is right for the team would consistently hold everyone back by missing their numbers. Pedal the Bike is an analogy; if there are five team members, the bike is built for five people. If everyone puts out equal effort, the ride is pretty easy; if even one person doesn't, then other riders must pick up the slack. Pretty soon the four people pedaling realize that the bike built for five would probably go faster with the four people who pedal if they don't have freeloading rider #5. The team will often help you either set #5 straight or work with you to get them off the team. Leaders who are good at hiring the right people and practice the team approach to KPI's will see the difference almost immediately.

Here's a real example of driving metrics that matter with a team approach. After three successful years as a managing director, I was promoted to a regional-vice-president post with four offices. WeCulture worked in one office, and this was a nice case study. Now we can see if it is something scalable. Three more offices — all with different challenges but one thing in common. Like the office I took three years earlier, this region had the lowest KPI's in the company. I met with the managing directors, and we agreed to get all four offices on common reporting. We changed to a team KPI system and put the focus on client meetings, outbound submittals, job orders, and closed deals. I never counted dials, connect calls, or "talk time." The change was almost immediate as local managers focused on activity that mattered and set goals by team. We held monthly competitions and used a point system, picking winning teams to keep things interesting.

In three months, we were meeting KPI's as a region, and by month six, we were in the top three regions for KPI's every week. The teams were majority Millennial, and as soon as we focused on a team approach, the numbers improved. Our Baby Boomers took to the team concept, and as they embraced the change, experienced staff were now leading by example. While we talk a lot about Millennials as their majority grows in the workforce, Baby Boomers have a lot to offer through expertise and experience to drive results. They cannot be ignored, and WeCulture includes them too.☺

There was an another benefit. As the teams improved, some individuals did not stand out to the others. Many resigned, or we had to part ways. This is for the best. No one should work for a company that does not share their core values. The teams in each office felt good about the turnover. How did we know? Because as we experienced turnover through this process, our staff was referring new hires to join the team. This reduced our time to hire and increased new colleague engagement because those joining the team were brought to us by a peer. As I interviewed candidates, they would sit with me and ask about WeCulture; it was now not only a means to drive financial results but a way to attract talent. I'm sharing this though no matter what you might think reading it. A moment of personal pride was when a candidate who came to interview me said, "I heard you are the father of WeCulture."

The region hired over forty-five people that year and turned over about twenty existing colleagues. The vast majority of the twenty employees we turned over were either underperforming or just did not fit the team model we were building. Did we make a few hiring mistakes along the way? Sure we did, but we did a great job retaining talented people. Before we were taking existing colleagues and working with them to adopt WeCulture. Now people joining the organization were coming to work here because they believed in it. Belief is powerful, and if someone already believes in your corporate culture, they will immediately adopt the core values and increase the chance of a successful hire exponentially. We will talk more about how to leverage WeCulture to attract the best people throughout the book.

CONNECT ENTERPRISE GOALS TO THE TEAM METRICS

So Millennials want to be part of something bigger, a greater purpose. How can we leverage this to drive KPI's in a positive way? Share enterprise results as appropriate. In *Ownership Thinking* by Brad Hams, this point is clearly made and can help businesses large and small. Two misconceptions can contribute to bad culture.

One is that people believe companies and owners make huge profits. In the book, the author talks about taking employee surveys to see if they understand net profit as a percentage of revenue, and the results were surprising. Most employees thought profit percentage was twenty to thirty percent — that is net profit, not gross profit. Some said as high as 50 percent. Take a plant worker, retail store clerk, or even floor manager. If these colleagues feel the company is taking this huge, double-digit profit while they get a static paycheck, it can seriously impact effort. WeCulture is about helping teams understand how their KPI activity contributes to the greater goal. A great way to level set expectations would be to disclose financial results in schedule meetings throughout the year. Once the team understands how their efforts impact the bottom line, it can be used as a motivator in good times and a rally point to focus specific KPI's when the business is falling behind. Think of a manufacturing plant. Maybe material waste is a high percentage of operating cost. If we show that to the teams on the factory floor, then when we focus on training and measuring material waste next quarter, employees will understand why. More importantly, now if we lower material waste, we can show the positive results next quarter and use the KPI as a motivator in a positive way. The team contributed to an enterprise goal and understands the impact to the greater good.

Second is the connection from a KPI to team results and how team results impact the enterprise. KPI's at the individual level and team level can have a cascading impact on the enterprise. In staffing if average candidates submitted per desk or team is down, then it does not matter how many job orders we have. Recruiting will miss their financial goals. The cascading effect is that the salespeople who depend on this KPI also will not have enough candidates to sell; they miss their goals. Now the office misses the goal, then the region and so on... Establishing this link up the chain and how individual activities can impact teammates and the organization can be leveraged to drive action. When the team exceeds the submittal goal, I often also show the uptick in activity on the sales team and how it impacted revenue. I have found that colleagues want this information once the connection is made.

Enterprise goals tied to team KPI's become a motivator no matter what the results are. In tough times, it is a rally point and can tie to a specific area of improvement. We make those KPI's the focus and measure and publish team results. In times of achievement, we show how the team KPI goals actually drove the success by tracing revenue back to specific moments in time. It proves out every time in staffing. Show me an eight- to twelve-week stretch of high candidate-submittal numbers, and four to eight weeks later we see a corresponding increase in revenue because we put more candidates to work.

USE INCENTIVES TO DRIVE BEHAVIOR

In sales this is easy. A sale for a sales professional equals income — the incentive is built in. Back to manufacturing and material waste. If material waste is hurting profits and can be impacted by a change in your employee activity, then provide an incentive to reach the goal. Share the challenge with your teams and give them the quantifiable impact of material waste. Next train on changes in the process to reduce waste. Quantify a team goal that will make a difference for the company financially and lastly offer the workers a percentage of the cost savings and share the win. Here is an example: Think about a company that manufactured corrugated boxes, a business with single-digit profit percentages. Material waste and rework on orders can have a serious impact on net income. A possible solution: training staff to ensure procedures were followed and setting a team goal for reduced material waste and orders reworked. The reward for employees: thirty cents of every dollar saved if the goal is hit each month. The goal should be tied to a significant reduction and must be an all-or-nothing proposition. If the team gets its bonus every month, the owner gets seventy cents of every dollar saved right to the bottom line. This is mutually assured value based on team effort from the business owner right down to the employee on the manufacturing floor.

By the way, when focusing on KPI's that matter with a team approach, we grew the business. All four years the businesses managed with WeCulture grew year over year and outpaced the company's overall growth by a substantial margin. We had low turnover, a strong culture where staff refer new hires, and significant year-over-year growth. Take a look at your business KPI's with your leadership team and ask yourself, what metrics are you measuring that yield results? Which metrics are outdated time wasters eroding culture and causing turnover? Quantify the time spent on these. If this time was spent on more meaningful, measurable activities that drive sales, what impact could this have on financial results for all?

WE INCLUDES LEADERS TOO

When it comes to KPI's, the team will look to you to lead by example. Nothing says team effort like working alongside the colleagues you are charged to lead. One of the biggest reasons teams fail to exceed KPI's is because management spends too much time telling their people what to do. In sales we see this all the time — sales managers who sit in offices and demand more activity without helping the team succeed.

I had a managing director who reported to me not too long ago, and his staff literally hated him. For a while I could not understand why, so I spent two weeks back-to-back in their branch office to observe the group dynamic. This MD was an experienced leader and came to us highly recommended. In our one-on-one meetings, he was confident and knew our business quite well. As I sat in on meetings, he spent lots of time providing good feedback, guidance on how to handle difficult situations, and had a keen eye to get to the heart of issues quickly. His communication style was direct and seemed effective, and as he spoke, I felt confident his judgement was sound. Meetings would end with a recap of action items by colleague — and then I had my answer. He never left a meeting with a to-do. The meeting would end, and he would retreat to his private office and close the door, leaving all the heavy lifting to his team. I thought this might be an exception, but after four days on site, I realized why the team hated this guy. He was all talk and no action.

The best way to get buy-in is to work with the team and demonstrate how to perform the job with personal action. Next time you host a team meeting, let a colleague lead it, and when action items are agreed to, make sure you personally have deliverables to help the team achieve the goal. Leading sales teams managing through other leaders, I still walk out of meetings with client-facing action items. I still do phone call blocks with the teams. If there is a difficult client call to make, I volunteer to do it myself. People learn by watching it happen and appreciate that I'm not "too important" to make calls.

Letting staff lead on special projects builds their skill sets. I never run charity team-building exercises — not ever. I do support my colleagues' charities, and when they invite me to participate, my role is to show up ready to work under their direction for the day. My office manager recently asked us to pack meals for a day at a food bank. The director on site saw we had a big team and asked us to clear out and reorganize the stockroom, and it was a total mess. I saw the look in my office manager's eyes when she asked for volunteers and I immediately raised my hand to get in the mix. It was by far the worst job, but two others joined me, and we took about nine hours to get it done. It was dark, and after clearing the shelves, we decided to clean each one and mop the floors. We are salespeople at heart and found a way to have a few laughs while working. My office manager loved having her RVP be her employee for the day, and the jokes never got old.

When it comes to hard work, "we" includes managers and senior leadership too. Get in the game and put a day of work in to show those you are charged to lead that you care. If you are a restaurant manager, clear a few tables if it gets busy. In a manufacturing plant? Keep your safety gear in the trunk of your car and be prepared to work on the line for a few hours if the team is feeling some pressure.

Pedaling the Bike cannot help the team win by itself. How we govern our actions through day-to-day work also sets the tone for good culture, which leads us to WeCulture Core Value #2.

"Successful entrepreneurs are givers and not takers of positive energy."

— Anonymous

CHAPTER FOUR

BE POSITIVE

As we get the business executing on activity, we need to fuel and channel our collective energy toward a common goal. How leaders carry themselves through each day can have a profound impact on the work environment. Millennials want to be part of something bigger than the work at their own desk. WeCulture's Core Value #2, Be Positive, can help your business thrive.

The Harvard Business Review did a survey in August 2015 ("The Top Complaints from Employees about Their Leaders" by Lou Solomon) on top employee complaints about bad bosses, and number one was "not recognizing employee achievements." The most telling common feedback about managers was "too much criticism and not enough praise." I have experienced firsthand working for or with thankless managers at all levels. Looking back at my own career and how human beings are motivated inside and outside of the workplace, positive energy is the spark toward change — the light at the end of a tunnel when times are tough. As we look at how core values can impact the work environment along with financial results, Be Positive becomes critical to sustaining meaningful progress. This sounds so simple, yet employee feedback says this lesson is largely ignored by leaders. This is because new managers are taught by the current leaders, and the energy of corporate culture is handed down. My manager will likely treat me the same way they are treated by theirs and so on. The study shows the perception by employees is that their boss is more focused on negative feedback than praise. Negative energy feeds a negative outlook and, in time, will have the same negative impact on financial results.

Spending eight years with a company where we focused the majority of our energy on what was wrong versus what was right about our business made me realize the change starts from within. We cannot wait for the company to change; as leaders or staff-level colleagues, we can be the spark to drive change. As we worked in our branch driving WeCulture to rebuild our business, we applied basic principles to our second core value (Be Positive) to break the cycle of negative energy. Negative people are corporate cancer. They settle in, make excuses, and fail to execute. As leaders tolerate this behavior, it spreads from desk to desk, and as we said before, our most talented people want to be on a winning team. They have choices in the market, and if the situation does not improve, they will leave the company. Once this happens, managers are left with only the worst performers, having a disastrous impact on results. Left untreated this can stop even the largest organizations dead in their tracks. Turnover is the largest non-line-item cost to any business. Lost productivity, search expenses, onboarding, training, and interruption to services can all be tied to hard costs. In sales, turnover can be devastating. Sales turnover also leads to lost clients on top of other costs, making growth almost impossible. If we go back to the top reasons people leave companies, it is usually a bad boss or poor culture. WeCulture works to address these issues at the source by giving leaders tools and guidance to create a positive workplace to retain employees. To help leaders focus, Be Positive has its own set of virtues. Leading people through people, I would often spend hours coaching managers and used these as a guide in all daily interactions.

THE RIGHT ENERGY STARTS WITH YOU

As already shared, I know who I bring to work every day. I'm the guy brushing his teeth every morning thinking, "How can today be a little better than yesterday?" While it starts there, it goes much deeper. As an RVP, I would travel from office to office each week, usually for a few days at a time. After leaving an office, I might not return for a few weeks; the impression I leave behind will count. If you can be known for anything as a leader, be known as the person who is a welcome sight to your teams. Make your very first action when you arrive meaningful. When walking in to an office, check your emotional and business baggage at the door. Had a fight with your spouse on the way in? Check this bag at the door. Had a tough call with the back office? Check this bag at the door too. No matter what was going on, I entered the office every day, took a deep breath, and greeted everyone with a smile. That usually got me lots of smiles back and some talk about things happening with colleagues as I went through the office going desk to desk. Positive energy makes you approachable, and the colleagues you are charged to lead will look to share the great things going on in the office. While we talk about good things going on at work, we are reinforcing the message that our company is a great place to work. Pretty soon the bags of negative energy I checked at the door were a distant memory.

Focus on things that are going right first to transfer positive energy to other colleagues. Negative energy is corporate cancer; positive energy is the cure. Catch a colleague doing something right. As we turned around a struggling office in my role as managing director discussed in chapter two, this was a tall order in the first few weeks on the job. We focused on even the smallest wins: a candidate submission to a new job, scheduling a visit with a new contact — all would get a "good job" at our daily job-order meetings. Encouraging small wins would lead to more activity. Genuine positive reinforcement of desired behavior brings more desired activity. The sparks take hold and will ignite the flame. Submissions became interviews, and interviews turned to candidates going to work (a sale). Your positive energy driving behavior toward the team goals. If you want your teams to do something consistently, give a sincere "good job" in the moment, preferably in public.

Case in point: My first sales hire in this office was struggling a bit and after three months got his first sale with a major retailer to upgrade its POS systems. It started with some basic encouragement as he hit his activity levels and scored one of his first meetings with this company. We worked together on the sale, but he found the client and drove home the win. We talked about how he found this customer at our next staff meeting, and this spark of recognition took him on a run to repeat the same process with several other new customers in the sector. As we talked about his first win in the meeting, he researched his client's competition and called each one, telling them the story of our first success. They quickly became some of our best clients. Eventually this became a win for the team as we built a practice around his success, which helped the delivery team put people to work. A small win recognized encouraged repeat behavior to create a multimillion-dollar practice for our business. No pushing, no prodding to get it done — just positive reinforcement and giving him the support along the way. The recognition from the team reinforced repeat behavior. A general rule of thumb: What the team recognizes will be repeated.

Lesson for every leader: Start every day with the one thing done right before you focus on anything done wrong. If you are really looking, finding something positive should happen quickly, putting the business on the way to a productive day.

WE CAN, NOT WE CAN'T

When faced with a difficult challenge, it is much easier to think of why we cannot than think of how we can. Colleagues at all levels get caught up in this regardless of their role in the company. If the team is geared toward starting with "we can't" because it is easier than actually working the problem, the person who needs help or the client might hear "we won't." In sales the translation of "we won't" for the customer usually becomes "I'll take my business to someone who will." "We can't" just became a lost client and lost revenue.

Take the example of a lost paycheck. The back-office procedure is to issue a stop payment, confirm this transaction, and then issue a new payment. This is days in lost time, and think about how the impact a delay in pay could mean to you for even a few days. Asking why helped me find out that approval from a manager could expedite an overnight, off-cycle check. Yes, it was some extra paperwork and a small cost to satisfy our candidate, but in this case, clearly "we can't" just required someone to ask what could be done to make a next-day payment possible. How can we say "we can"?

Incredible and impossible things will happen when people have the right attitude thinking "we can." Leaders can inspire, and history holds examples of vision becoming reality. President John F. Kennedy inspired our nation to put men on the moon in 1962 during an address at Rice University on September 12. The commitment to have men on the moon before the end of the decade seemed impossible at the time. NASA did not have the resources, and as a nation, we were far behind the Soviets in the steps needed to achieve this daunting goal. The U.S. was losing the space race to the then-Soviet Union and had yet to successfully launch an American astronaut into space. The spark of "we can" triggered one of man's greatest achievements and rallied the expansion of NASA. Our nation began thinking of all the steps needed to make this impossible goal become a reality: Project Apollo. After a series of eleven Apollo missions, Neil Armstrong and Buzz Aldrin landed on the moon on July 20, 1969, making Kennedy's vision a reality.

Today NASA has project Orion and looks on to Mars. This started with a great leader saying "we can."

Anytime you are confronted with "we can't," the next question should be why. WeCulture's approach to "we can't" is to post the "impossible goal" on the board and partner with the team to break down all the things that need to happen to make the impossible possible. What is the first step toward the goal? If this step is possible, what is the next possible step heading toward the goal? Keep outlining the steps in the meeting until the last step makes the goal possible. Once the team figures out something can be done, let's assign the tasks along the way and get there. It is a matter of simple project management and not accepting "we can't" at face value when you hear it. Nothing motivates the team more than achieving a common goal (especially when the initial reaction is that the goal is unachievable). Including the people who said it could not be done will help you reshape how they look at business challenges for the future; next time they will start with "we can."

Sounds easy? Tune in to your colleagues with this in mind and see where your culture stands and keep a log. Is your corporate culture one based on can't or can? A quote from Confucius, an ancient Chinese philosopher: "He who says he can and he who says he can't are both usually right." This will stand true for how we lead. WeCulture teaches leaders to encourage "we can."

RECOGNIZE POINTS OF FAILURE AS OPPORTUNITY

Things will go wrong; it is inevitable. The ability to work with teams to solve complex problems is a true skill that can be learned. How we handle problems as a leader will absolutely shape employee behavior. Be Positive is a core value that can encourage honesty and teamwork when things go wrong, and the truth is, when there is a critical problem, "we" includes you more than ever. Here Pedal the Bike alone is not enough; the energy a leader displays speaks louder than action. Let's start by accepting that our business would be more successful if we catch problems early on while they are small. A leak in a dam can become a catastrophic failure left unchecked. In business a simple problem like improper invoicing can frustrate a client and send them to your competition. If we knew about an invoicing issue the first cycle and corrected the situation, it would be like it never happened. In staffing, our product is people. The list of things that can go wrong is almost endless. How do we encourage colleagues to bring problems to us?

In WeCulture executive leaders should be coaching and mentoring managers on how to handle day-to-day challenges. Your reaction in a challenging situation speaks volumes about your character, and those you are charged to lead will take notice. Future behavior on how colleagues react when faced with a challenge are reinforced for better or worse. Putting the client first with a solution focus as the primary goal allows everyone to take a clinical approach needed for effective problem solving. The focus on pride, ego, and blame all take away from energy on meaningful work.

While rebuilding our business, I was partnered with the national accounts team on two of our large clients. Anytime a problem would arise, their response was focused on who was responsible, how could something like this happen, and consequences associated with the point of failure. Every interaction would take time spent on hearing how bad things were before we could get toward solving the issue at hand. Aside from wasted time, when blame is the focus, employees will spend energy spinning or hiding critical information that might be helpful to solve the problem. Blame is another form of culture cancer. The spin cycle to avoid blame promotes a dishonest undertone to the team that will erode trust. Once the trust is gone, people will stop working together and, in extreme cases, work against each other internally. Finger-pointing takes center stage ahead of the challenge at hand. The sales team would often avoid bringing even small challenges to the national account team as a result. For our business, this created risks; problems don't sit well and rarely go away on their own. Lose a national account, and it can take years for the company to recover. We needed to reshape our approach fast.

We had one of our account managers, an eight-year veteran, get caught on a client-procedure violation that, to our contact, seemed intentional. The call came from the national account VP, and we spent an hour on a call talking about consequences for the local account manager. I got a second call from my SVP saying how horrible this looked and asking over and over how we could allow this to happen. All blame, all we-are-screwed, all not focused on the client. Two days later a third call with a few more senior leaders from the national accounts team and enough was enough. I asked if we could talk about a solution to the problem and deal with consequences for the account manager later. We agreed I would visit the client with the national account VP. All the talk was of firing the account manager who had been with us for eight years and how egregious the mistake was. For three days, we made our client wait for communication while we discussed this nonsense. We saw the client and in a forty-five-minute meeting were able to solve the problem. The client agreed that while a mistake was made, things happen in business. It was an easy fix while we spent days speculating consequences, discussing blame, making our client wait and creating unnecessary risk, all while alienating our eight-year veteran who had grown the account from day one. Once we were all focused on a solution, the problem was solved with a twenty-minute internal discussion and a visit to the client office. By the way, the account manager who made this mistake brought it to our attention, not the client. That account manager never trusted the major-accounts team again.

For difficult situations, WeCulture manager coaching is simple: A problem is an opportunity to help your colleagues. In the process, working together will build the bond with those you are charged to lead. Focus on the solution first. The "oh my God" moment should last five seconds. We are here — let's deal with it and work together. Combining "we can" with a solution-first approach will encourage colleagues to share all the information you need to solve a problem. Forget mistakes made that got us here. Focus on helping the colleagues involved solve the problem and put your client first. Solve a client problem quickly, and often it will solidify the relationship. Clients judge vendors based on how they handle tough situations, and you will need your team to help you make the pain go away.

Once the problem is solved or the fire is out, everyone involved will be more levelheaded for the next step. Do a post-mortem to figure out how and what happened. This is absolutely necessary to the success of the team and will help you hold people accountable, without the heat of battle to cloud your judgement. If colleagues made honest mistakes, use it as a teaching moment to build your relationship. Let them help you find a gap in a procedure and work on fixing it together. Thank them for their work to solve the problem and let them know how much you appreciate that they brought the issue to your attention. This encourages people to bring problems to you immediately. If colleagues come to you early, almost any problem can be solved. You will also spend less time auditing and looking for issues and more time driving the business. Exceptions here where consequences come into play would be blatant employment-policy violations, gross negligence, or unethical behavior. For me all violations of trust need to be addressed with appropriate measures and could include termination. Yes, in the chapter on Be Positive, we are discussing a possible outcome of termination. We are still running a business, and breach of trust is a deal breaker in WeCulture (more on this in chapter five).

BE SINCERE AND BE YOURSELF

As WeCulture takes hold and we execute on the core value of Be Positive, it is critical that behavior is sincere. Shifting focus over to emphasis on positive behavior to motivate the team will drive colleagues to repeat desired behaviors as long as we don't fake it. Going back to a book that changed my outlook on business, *True North* by Bill George, another key takeaway is to always be yourself. We interact with our colleagues at work every day and some more than our own family members. If we are not true to our own character, eventually the team will catch on. If our behavior is perceived as dishonest, it will erode trust and the culture with it.

I'm a born-bred, bonus-fed sales professional. A smile comes naturally to me, and my outlook is optimistic. I high-five our wins, and an occasional fist pump is not out of character for me. This core value comes easily to me and is seen as genuine when we celebrate success. During the rebuild of the region as we rolled out WeCulture, I hired a recruiting director in one of the struggling offices. He was a true-blue, big-city guy. Not a big high-fiver — very direct and matter of fact, regardless of the situation. You might be thinking he struggled with our core value of Be Positive. The truth is he did not; he actually excelled, and his people loved him. Why? His actions, words, and disposition toward problem-solving was always client-focused and "we can." Even without a smile and the stereotypical extrovert personality, he pulled it off because he was true to himself. The team respected him for who he was — his helpful nature, knowledge shared, and positive approach with quiet dignity. Be Positive is not about manufactured enthusiasm; it is about how we interact with colleagues, solving problems with a glass-half-full approach and having a "we can" disposition to our daily work.

Employee engagement and employee relations are fast becoming the trend for companies. The war for talent is heating up, and Baby Boomers retire at the rate of ten thousand people per day. Keeping the right talent is more critical than ever. Millennials replacing Baby Boomers come with a host of different expectations and being part of a "we can," team-oriented culture is at the top of their list of expectations of employers. While Be Positive is Core Value #2, I believe this is most important and is the fuel keeping colleagues engaged, productive, and working as a team toward company goals. This brings us to Core Value #3, Honest and Ethical.

"Waste no more time arguing about what a good man should be...be one."

— Marcus Aurelius

CHAPTER FIVE

HONEST AND ETHICAL

How we carry ourselves and the actions we take define who we are to the people we interact with regardless of the situation. The saying that goes, "You never get a second chance to make a first impression," stands true. I grew up around firemen, and they used to joke with me that "one 'aww shit' can ruin a million pats on the back from the chief." As a parent, I share the lesson with my children that one lapse in judgement can change your life forever. In the business world, the media loves a great scandal; clients have options and are unforgiving. Factor in that over the past decade social media has taken center stage, giving everyone we interact with a platform to share their experiences, and even with the best of intentions, perception becomes reality. A focus on honest and ethical behavior by companies is needed now more than ever. Doing the right thing always matters, which is why WeCulture's Core Value #3 is Honest and Ethical.

Here is an example of how unethical behavior can be self-destructive, leaving a wake of broken people and careers. In October 2001, Enron Corporation was brought to its knees, shocking the market and leaving employees stunned, with only their personal belongings as they left headquarters. Enron was once hailed as a leader in innovation for the energy industry, and its demise came as executive leaders modified balance sheets to show more favorable results. In addition to cooking the books, questionable energy-trading practices inflated profits to unprecedented levels. In an industry where 2- to 3-percent growth rates were the norm, Enron averaged 65 percent per year, quickly becoming a top ten company on the Fortune Global 500. In March 2001, an article in *Fortune* was published: "Is Enron Overpriced" by Bethany McLean. At the time, Enron's stock-trading value was fifty-five times its earnings. This all started as McLean viewed the company's 10-K report and found discrepancies in cash flow and transaction reporting. Then came an avalanche of attention from the media and Wall Street analysts that exposed one of the greatest scams in U.S. history. On October 16, 2001, Enron restated earnings for years 1997 to 2000 for accounting violations to the tune of over $600 million. Soon after, Enron went bankrupt.

Arthur Andersen was Enron's audit firm and part of the "Big Five." These public accounting and audit firms would certify the financial results of the largest companies in the world. A handful of individuals for Arthur Andersen participated in this large-scale scandal, and the company was convicted of obstruction of justice on June 15, 2002, for shredding documents related to its audit of Enron. Later that same year, Arthur Andersen, one of the most prestigious names in the world of accounting and audit, surrendered its licenses to practice as certified public accountants. Clients outside of the audit practices abandoned the firm, and it was literally willed out of existence in the market — all because of the unethical actions of one team, the Enron account. Thousands of honest, ethical, hardworking people had their careers and lives changed forever, and the company's $9.3 billion empire collapsed.

While this example seems like something that could never happen again, the real estate crash of 2008 was caused by greed and inflated ratings of mortgage-backed securities. The list can go on, but let's focus on how Honest and Ethical can drive results for the business if colleagues truly embrace this critical core value.

LEADERSHIP BEST PRACTICES

Managers and senior leaders set the tone, and actions will speak louder than words. The days of "Do as I say, not as I do" are long gone. If we expect those we are charged to lead to behave honestly and ethically, then we must be the example at all times. WeCulture only works if every level of the organization recognizes the three core values and displays them in everyday actions. The most talented individual contributors often fail to make the best leaders because they do not represent through personal action how they direct their subordinates. When this happens, the team will view the leader as dishonest or a hypocrite, eroding trust and overall effort. If there are rules, the best way to build trust and get others to follow is to hold yourself accountable first. Codes of conduct, recommended dress, and standard operating procedures need to be followed by all to have true meaning. The best leaders and business owners will not use their positions to avoid accountability. The rule here is if you believe, if you say, you should do.

One of the greatest military leaders in history was Hannibal. General of the Carthaginian army, he marched on the Roman Empire in 218 B.C. during the Second Punic War and won victory after victory on the Italian peninsula. Hannibal was known as a soldier's general. He did not live in luxury or lead battles from a hilltop. He lived as his soldiers lived, ate the same provisions, and fought alongside them in almost every battle. Hannibal set the tone for his armies through his own actions and led from the front, terrorizing all of Rome and routing its best generals in battle — all accomplished while leading by example and leading from the front.

Keep your word. If you say you are going to do something, make sure you do it. As we work toward the company goals, it will require teamwork. When I was promoted to RVP and expanding WeCulture to the new offices, I came across a managing director who was losing his team. To find out why, I spent more time at this office. This leader did not keep his word. We would have our daily job-order meeting, and he would take action items, committing to have them done by the end of the day. Many of these items were simple tasks, calls to provide support, or to simply make himself available to the team. The next day we would have our meeting, and the team would find out there was no follow-up. After excuses as to why and promises it would be the next item on the list, without action colleagues were often left without support or forced to fend for themselves. Aside from eroding trust, the team saw him as lazy or incompetent.

In another office, we had a leader recently promoted from a production role who moved in from another market. Taking his family clear across the country and working with a new team, he was able to grow the business every year and had little to no turnover. His team would execute because he would commit to action items and follow through with immediate communication on the outcome. He sat with his team in the bullpen and only used his office for private meetings. He made calls to clients and stayed late to help fill job orders when needed. His colleagues trusted him because his actions spoke, and he kept his word. Honest and ethical leadership reduced turnover, and together the team grew the business. His year-over-year growth was over 80 percent top-line revenue.

Let your team shine — give them all the credit when you win and take all the responsibility when things go wrong. While leading from the front is critical to success, the best leaders step aside and let their team enjoy the spotlight when there is a big win. As a leader, your job is to motivate and inspire others to execute, and when that effort yields the desired results, it needs to be all about the team. Public recognition is the key to positive reinforcement of desired behavior. When leaders take the credit for a job well done, team members may see the win as a negative. Forget those who helped you achieve success, and they will harbor resentment, another form of culture cancer. More often than not, colleagues will walk away quietly and share with their colleagues later how you hogged the spotlight or ignored their contributions. If this happens often enough, you may find your colleagues secretly working against you. Be aware of those around you; at project presentations, let the team have the spotlight to present whenever possible and always recognize those who contribute behind the scenes. While I was the managing director building WeCulture, our operations specialist helped us achieve 100 percent on every quarterly operational audit. This is not an exaggeration; the grade was 100 percent every time. These audits are only shared with her and me on the call with the audit team. Unless we shared this with the rest of our office, who would know? All of her hard work would go unrecognized. Everything she does to protect the business by meeting standard operating procedures on placements would go unnoticed. Her contributions to protect the team were a critical part of our success. After every audit, I would ask her to join the office meeting and share the results herself. I would also email our SVP and COO, sharing her good performance, which would bring a flood of congratulations from her peers around the country. By the way, our goal of every colleague making more money than last year? We included her too. Every year her performance allowed me to request the top percentage salary increase.

Things will go wrong even with flawless execution or the best intentions. When this happens, stand in front and take the heat. As the leader, you are ultimately responsible for everything that happens for the team. Your job is to keep everything on track and be ready to act if there is a problem. Service failure? Buffer your sales professional and call the client to apologize on behalf of the company. The salesperson's client relationship will sometimes need support, and in hard times, this is absolutely where "we" includes you. An honest mistake was made by a colleague that cost the company money? Help your colleague work to fix the error and take the heat. A project is not completed on time? A production goal not met? Take the heat. The reality is you are ultimately responsible anyway. Blame has no place in WeCulture and, as we said in the last chapter, a form of culture cancer. If someone on the team was negligent, talk with them about the mistakes made in private and handle the situation with appropriate corrective action.

Accept feedback and be willing to change. Being intellectually honest with yourself means accepting you are not perfect. During one-on-ones, ask your colleagues for constructive, professional feedback on how you can personally improve performance to help the team win. There are times where you may have questions on how a message was received. Maybe the team seems a bit off their game. Maybe numbers are down. The first thing you can control is your own actions, and the people you are charged to lead can share great insight. If you thank people for critical feedback and follow through with changes in behavior, it will cement the bond you have with rest of the group. You can learn a lot about yourself — open your mind, close your mouth, and listen. The best professional feedback can come from your direct reports; after all, they have the most exposure to how you manage your own behavior.

At times this will require you to admit when you are wrong. Ego becomes the enemy here. Most people have trouble admitting they are wrong in a peer situation; here we are saying leaders should embrace being wrong and admit it. Do this, and you will be seen as someone who is self-aware, honest, and ethical. Being wrong is not a sign of weakness; failure to admit when you make mistakes is. Once you admit a mistake, an honest, good-faith effort to get back on track will be welcomed by your colleagues. It sets a tone that there is a level playing field and that you embody the same traits expected of them. This will help establish and maintain trust, which is the foundation of any relationship. The faster you recognize and admit a mistake, the faster we get to a solution.

Don't make promises unless you are sure you can deliver. First-time managers often make this mistake, overestimating relationships with the back office or senior leadership. "I'm sure I can convince legal to accept these contract changes." Are you really sure or just confident? More often than not, this misstep is unintentional. At best your team sees you as honest but not experienced enough to know better. At worst it is viewed as a lie. Either outcome will cause colleagues to lose faith in your ability to lead. Use language that clearly states intent and only commit to something if you are the sole decision maker. Instead of promising you can get a contract change through, you can say you are confident but not 100 percent sure.

Be prepared to do anything you would ask a teammate to do. I believe this goes without saying, and anyone who does not believe this should not be charged to lead. Remember back in chapter two when I was the managing director over a failing business trying to establish WeCulture? Well that office was also a physical mess, an eyesore. Boxes everywhere, equipment stacked in empty cubicles, paint scuffed walls, and the office refrigerator — if only I had taken a few pictures. How could we attract top talent to work there if the office looked like that? A messy office says, "People don't care about this place." We agreed to clean the office up as a team and stay late once a week until it was done. As we cleaned out the fridge, we washed it clean together. We collected bulk trash items and took them to the dumpster together. I worked with our ops manager to do a file purge and shredded expired documents with her. We cleaned scuffs off the paint. Once it was clean, we agreed to keep it that way and did. Everyone was willing to do these undesirable jobs to improve the office environment; I was no different. When it comes to the dirtiest jobs, "we" includes you too.

Deliver constructive feedback in a timely manner. Radical candor is a theme I hear a lot used by executives and is often abused in practice. It becomes a means to deliver critical feedback with little concern for the colleague on the receiving end. Let's start with a few things radical candor is not. It is not a blank check to be unprofessional, use foul language, personally attack another colleague, or make the situation about ego. Radical candor is about delivering constructive or critical feedback with intention of helping colleagues be better for the team. Your peers, subordinates, and those who are charged to lead all improve through their ability to process feedback regarding performance. If people are wrapped up in their personal feelings or ego, any hope of progress is lost. WeCulture's core value, Honest and Ethical, is designed to encourage internal interaction where transparency is welcome. Our personal pride has no place in WeCulture; issues are dealt with in a clinical way, putting the client or solution first. Don't allow ego to slow the team down.

In meetings radical candor can be used to great effect to vet issues and risks associated with projects. The book *Five Dysfunctions of a Team* by Patrick Lencioni says two critical breakdowns in teamwork are driven by "Absence of Trust" and

"Fear of Conflict." A lack of honesty in meetings would feed a false sense of harmony and create cliques among the team. Often little would be accomplished in the actual meeting because the issue preventing meaningful progress would never be discussed. Worse was the culture of the "Meeting after the Meeting," where participants would go to privately lobby for resources or make their points to senior leadership. When leaders allow this behavior, they feed a cycle of dishonesty and fear. Maybe a project has merit, but "my boss will entertain private discussion after a meeting, I'll hold my thoughts until then." We have already established withholding information is the same as a lie. Because of a lack of honesty, little would get done, and the corporate cancer of politics would take hold. Poor leadership feeds this problem, and executives take sides and allow their egos to guide decisions. A great tactic to prevent the "Meeting after the Meeting": When a colleague enters your office and begins lobbying or talking about an issue that concerns someone else, always invite the other team members back to the table. Your colleagues will catch on quickly. My favorite cure quote to finish a meeting to evaluate consensus: "Last chance for input. Remember, in WeCulture there is no meeting after the meeting."

HONEST AND ETHICAL TO DRIVE RESULTS

The story of Arthur Andersen shows how unethical behavior for a single client can bring down one of the largest global organizations. Granted, the impact of its unethical behavior was substantial, but it illustrated the point. Let's talk about how honest and ethical behavior can build a reputation to drive results and retain the best talent.

Social media has become the go-to place for information on companies, goods, and services. Mobile apps like Glassdoor share reviews of employers posted by employees and are now considered a reputable source for inside information. Candidates who go on interviews will use this as one of many sources to evaluate job opportunities. Facebook has become a platform for anyone to share experiences large and small. YouTube will post almost any video shot on a mobile device for anyone in the world who wants to see it. The list goes on. If how we conduct business is held to a high standard, we can leverage honest and ethical behavior to build the company reputation toward driving sales.

LinkedIn is one of the most well-known and recognized professional-networking, social media outlets in the world. With over 450 million active users, its platform is geared toward business interaction. In staffing this is a primary tool for communication with candidates and client contacts — often a point of first contact. Think about what staffing companies actually do. We help people find jobs, or if they already have a job, the goal is to get them a better one. Most people spend the majority of their waking hours at work, and changing jobs is a difficult decision even under ideal circumstances. Because of this, honesty in our business is key to prolonged success. Get someone a better job or a job if they are unemployed, and you can change his or her life. If that job turns out to be everything the recruiter said it would be, candidates will appreciate the experience and share it. Recommendations from a candidate placed to recruiters is common on LinkedIn and helps build market creditability. Profiles with posted recommendations for service performed are eight times more likely to generate sales-related activity. More activity yields more candidates and client contacts and will lead to results.

I love recruiting. When people ask me what I do for a living, I'm very proud of the career I chose. If we do our job using honesty and ethics to drive behavior every time we make a sale, someone gets a job. After almost twenty years, along with the people I have been charged to lead, we have found countless people great jobs. WeCulture helps bring ethics to the forefront of selling for our team. When teams put honesty first, you might lose a sale today and gain a client for a career. When Millennials evaluate companies, they look for the opportunity to be part of the greater good — ethics to attract the right talent. Aside from driving business — helping us hire and retain good people — I put my head on the pillow every night with a clear head. At times doing the right thing can be hard. It takes admitting a mistake or that you were wrong. It means core values come before short-term gains or how things might look in the moment. First-order consequences are the short-term impact of a decision and usually motivated by pride or ego. It takes every colleague to remain vigilant and hold each other accountable. This core value truly requires leadership to set the standard to ensure honest and ethical behavior first and then be followed by all.

As a staff-level colleague, you can drive this core value and reinforce it each day. Being honest and ethical yourself is a great place to start, but it does not end there. The vast majority of people are honest and ethical and will withhold information or lie if motivated by fear of consequences. This can be to cover an honest mistake: something easy to fix, a case where the lie to cover it up does more damage for the long term. Dishonesty is another form of culture cancer. The best way to promote Core Value #3 is for every colleague to be solution-focused. Accept that your peers, managers, and subordinates will make mistakes. When mistakes happen, regardless of the cause, all colleagues should work together to solve the problem at hand. How we got to where we are can be dealt with after we work together to find a solution. As colleagues you must fight the urge to judge your peers and work to help them when facing a challenge. If people truly believe the team will support them when facing a problem or challenge (even if they were negligent), they are more likely to be honest. No need to cover up a problem if you can count on your colleagues to help you solve it.

If you see something, say something. You can hold your peers accountable and encourage them to do the right thing in the moment. This is hard for people to accept and even harder to do in practice, but the motivation is that the actions of your colleagues will impact the work environment. With all of the time you spend at work, accept that you create the culture. Think of the example of Arthur Andersen we discussed earlier in this chapter. If colleagues at the time reported the unethical behavior of the team assigned to Enron, Arthur Andersen would still be in business. For the short term, its reputation may have been damaged, but it would have cemented trust that its culture puts ethical behavior first. This is not about running to your manager to report on your peers; it is about talking to them in the moment and coaching them in a positive way to make the right decision — maybe reminding them not to shortcut a procedure, encouraging them to step forward when they make a mistake, or helping them in the moment if they lack the skill or experience to get something right. Be the spark that promotes ethical behavior.

Looking beyond the corporate world, think about how important Honest and Ethical behavior can impact community trust in civil servants. Law enforcement professionals have one of the hardest jobs in the world and are often held to a very high standard. Their job is to protect about 98 percent of the population from the other 2 percent who might do harm to society. In performing their duties, they issue tickets for violations of the law and, at times, must use force to protect themselves and the public. Many decisions are made in the heat of the moment, yet actions are analyzed over and over again. Law enforcement counts on the trust of the people to perform its job effectively. Building this trust is done by each officer holding to a high standard of ethical behavior at all times. All it takes is a few dishonest officers to erode trust for the entire department, and the impact could have dire consequences for the rest of the team.

This is a very controversial topic. Without using a specific example, ask yourself: If a local law enforcement officer in your town had to use force to defend himself or herself, based on the department's current reputation, does the officer get the benefit of a doubt? Or is the action viewed with public outrage? Would the action be accepted as necessary or would there be a protest? The behavior of each officer will create a collective reputation to build or undermine trust and public confidence. In the corporate world, lack of trust undermines financial results; for law enforcement, the stakes are much higher. For government and civil servants, core values to govern behavior can save lives, keep teams safe, and impact the behavior of the public beyond their organization.

Now that we have our core values to guide behavior, we can move on best practices. How does WeCulture help us find, evaluate, attract, and retain the best talent? Can we leverage WeCulture and adapt it to your business? Can we use this to drive results? What impact can standard operating procedures have to drive culture? How do we change the behavior of existing staff and tenured managers? What are the tools we can use to guide us along the way? How can WeCulture be customized to a specific business?

"A strategy, even a great one, doesn't implement itself."

— *Jeroen De Flander*

DRIVE SUCCESS THROUGH ENGAGEMENT AND EXECUTION

"Great vision without great people is irrelevant."
— Jim Collins

CHAPTER SIX
THE RIGHT TALENT

The foundation of any successful business starts with the right people. Sure, if you are a small-business owner, your personal drive and determination can overcome any shortfall in hiring because you are able to influence the business directly. But as success takes hold and your small business grows, having the right people becomes critically important to fuel growth. People who share a vision of success are not enough; the path they choose to achieve success must be aligned with yours. Your employees represent your brand, product, or service, and in today's unforgiving business climate, their actions can make or break what has been built. Think of all the hard work it takes to win clients and then consider how easily one can be lost. Core values must be set to govern behavior. How can we know if someone is the right hire? As discussed in chapter two, while developing WeCulture in our office, the business grew rapidly. We started to hire aggressively to fuel sales and sustain the pace. Now that we had WeCulture in place, I realized that who we hire is critically important, so we evaluated the hiring process to help ensure success. Who creates the culture? We all do...and "we" includes the newbies too.

I began working with a colleague, and over a few meetings, we outlined the company's current hiring process. We also looked at company turnover stats — over 70 percent. Even for a staffing company, this rate of turnover was crippling our business and well above the stated target goal of 30 percent. If we are going to examine the hiring process, we must evaluate why turnover is so high. This requires an introspective look. Employee turnover is something every manager at all levels of the organization will face throughout his or her career. Regardless of the reasons — termination or resignation — the timing is almost never right, and the cost of hiring and training new staff can really hurt productivity and the team. Identifying and interviewing candidates can take weeks. Combine this with ramp-up time and chronic turnover can put the team behind budget, have a serious impact on morale, and really impact results. Aside from the stress for you, your colleagues, and the organization, this can be a bonus killer...maybe even career stunting. If you own a small to midsize business, turnover can be a disaster.

Leading teams partnering with frontline managers, I have heard many reasons for turnover, and more often than not, managers put turnover on the candidate. "They were not willing to put the work in," "not a culture fit," "were not catching on to training," "did not get along with the group," "lacked attention to details"...the list goes on and on. Unless turnover happens because of life circumstance, health issues, family, or someone wins the lottery, these are symptoms of the two real, underlying reasons for turnover. The best leaders look at their own behavior first and own up to the part they played in losing an employee. After we put ego aside, turnover boils down to two reasons: failure to hire the right person or failure to motivate the right person. Both reasons are on the company and the leadership.

An introspective look is hard, but if you are intellectually honest, this will be a call to action for change. Knowledge is power — facing the truth about what you can do better will help you be a more effective leader to attract and retain the best people. Once we established a need for action through a review of current status versus goal and accepted that we are responsible for the success of hires, we moved on to a review of our hiring process. Together we did a whiteboard exercise outlining all the steps taken to attract and evaluate talent.

As we walked through the process, we started with how we find people. Like most companies, we count on referrals and are dependent on job descriptions to describe the role we are looking to fill. Most job descriptions include a paragraph about the company (usually prepared by marketing or HR), along with a long-winded description of duties and required skills. Resumes come in through a portal or are sent by a recruiter for review, and we evaluate a candidate's skills, work history, and achievements against our job description to decide if we would invite candidates in for an interview. This process is common across industries, and we were no different. As we continued the discussion, we looked at our interview process and how we evaluated talent. We had interview teams by department and gave each colleague specific things to look for. Typically we reviewed the resume, asking about past jobs to see how those skills aligned with ours. Some colleagues were better than others about asking for specific accomplishments in a candidate's work history. As we rounded out the list, the results were clear. Our teams were trained to evaluate talent based on skills acquired through experience. Sounds great, right? Find a person who has done a similar role along with the skills we need, and we have our hire.

As we started to look at people who had left the firm, our discussion took an interesting turn. Many of the individuals hired had the right work history and skills. This was no surprise since our hiring process was almost exclusively focused on hard skills. If people had the right quantitative experience making them capable of doing the job, then why were they leaving? By the time we got to our tenth colleague who had left, the answer was clear. Without exception, regardless of termination or resignation, the reasons always tied back to core values and core qualities. If core values and core qualities are so critical to success, we would need to rethink how we identify and evaluate talent.

We started with a simple overview of what we would interview for based on the needs of the job and stack ranked level of importance based on our discussion. Our interviews would now be designed to screen applicants based on the below four categories:

1. WeCulture Core Values
2. Desired Core Qualities
3. Skills
4. Accomplishments

EVALUATING CORE VALUES

Incorporating WeCulture into the interview process changes how we look at hiring. How do we screen for Pedal the Bike, Be Positive, and Honest and Ethical to find out if a potential hire shares these basic values? With our core values defined, we started to create questions that could be asked in an interview to help understand how a potential hire might fit the culture. There is absolute art and science to this. Questions used can be situational or about specific, past, work-related experience. For Pedal the Bike, I would ask potential applicants what their last job had for key performance indicators. I would then move on to understand how they were measured, what the actual quantifiable goals were for each, and, lastly, how did they measure up when stack ranked in their peer group. That's an example of a simple line of questioning that would help us determine if this person would Pedal the Bike. For Be Positive, we would ask questions about difficult situations in a past role, how these situations arise, and steps the team would take to solve a problem. We asked applicants, how would you handle a mistake made by a colleague? Tell me about a time something at work did not go your way. What was the situation? Who was involved? How did you react? What was the outcome? Honest and Ethical: Tell me about a time you lost a sale. What happened, and what was your part in it? Share your last experience where you had to share bad news with your manager. What was the situation? Outcome? What we are looking for here is, will a candidate avoid canned, "spin" answers and own up. The ability to admit when mistakes are made is a sign of confidence and ethical behavior.

DEFINING AND SCREENING FOR CORE QUALITIES

Core qualities are the desired traits we look for that are common to the most successful people in our organization. Our list of desired core qualities is intelligence, communication skills, thought process, and drive. How do we come up with a list of key core qualities? Host a meeting with your senior leaders and make a list on a whiteboard of your best seven to ten colleagues. After you list these individuals, have each person walk up to the board and put an adjective to describe his or her best quality next to the name. The next step is to look for common ground among the individuals listed. Any of the adjectives that are listed once should be erased immediately. Anything listed multiple times should be discussed with the goal in mind that the group come up with three to five desired core qualities to look for in their hires. Once you have a list, this will become the basis of what we look for in potential hires. Why? Because these are the core qualities of our most valued current staff. Like shared core values, if people share similar core qualities, they should work well together. Core values are timeless and govern behavior; core qualities are almost impossible to learn. Skills can be taught. Which should come first, the intangible things we cannot teach that are critical to the success of the organization or a skill that we can teach someone?

To illustrate the point, let's discuss the core qualities we used in our business. Intelligence, we agreed, is someone's ability to acquire and apply knowledge and is valued to help new hires learn quickly. Communication skills measures how well candidates can communicate their thoughts in a clear and concise manner. In sales or recruiting, this is critical to success and building relationships. Thought process is how an individual can solve a complex problem or how they perform under pressure. I believe we see who people really are when they are outside their comfort zones. Drive is most important. This is the undefinable inner force that makes you perform at your best. It is self-motivation, the voice that says, "I want to win." This is what separates people who succeed from those who do not in a similar circumstance. These are the people who have displayed throughout their career and life choices the attitude of "I can." Below are sample questions used to measure our desired core qualities:

Intelligence:
- Tell me about the last complex process you learned and explain how it works, knowing I may need to learn it myself.
- What is a subject in college you had to work harder at than others? Why?
- How did your compensation plan work in your last job? (Does the candidate have a clear understanding of it?)
- Interviewer should explain a concept, such as gross profit, basic technology, or the recruiting model, and gauge a candidate's ability to comprehend at a basic level.
- How did your last employer make money?
- What is your style of learning?

Communication skills:
- What types of people do you find it difficult to work with? How do you handle it?
- Share a success you had in your last job.
- Tell me about a time when you had to explain a difficult or complex idea to someone? How did you handle it?
- Tell me about a time when you had to voice an idea or opinion that you knew may be controversial or unpopular.

- Describe the work-environment culture and communication style you need to be successful in an organization.
- Can you describe your current sales process?
- Tell me about the value proposition for your current product or service.

Thought process:
- Tell me about a sale (or business success) you are proud of. Why?
- What was the first job you ever had? What did you learn from it about the work world?
- Tell me how you chose your college and major? Would you change your choice now that you have graduated and entered the workforce? Why?
- How did you choose your first job after graduating from college? How did the role match up to your expectations? Why did you move on?
- Why staffing? Why our company?
- How do you like to be held accountable?
- Tell me about something you did in college or the professional world that did not go well. What action did you take? What was your part in it going wrong? How did you fix it? What did you learn from it?
- Who in your work history made a lasting impression on you? Why? How did it impact choices you make today?

Drive:
- How do you rank in your current peer group?
- Where did you rank in your last two jobs?
- How many people had the same role as you for each of these jobs?
- What do you do each day that goes beyond what is expected?
- Tell me about a time where you won a new client where persistence was needed? What were your actions that made the difference?
- Why do people buy from you?

How people answer these questions can offer insight into their character and how they would fit in with WeCulture. In staffing we often hire candidates who are new to their careers. While the situational questions above related to work history might be a great approach for experienced applicants, recent graduates have little work experience to tap into. For these hires, we must dig deeper. I believe that an individual's core values and core qualities are formed during high school and the two to three years after. Experiences early on shape how we view the world and will often govern how we handle situations in the future. My line of questioning usually starts with the first job they ever had. I don't care how old they were or what the job was. What I'm really looking for is the lesson they took from the experience. As I introduced myself in this book, we looked back on my work history through high school and college. The lessons I took from the experience early on shaped my outlook as I entered the professional world and impacted performance. From here I ask questions about high school:

- Where did you attend high school?
- What did you do in school besides attend classes?
- What did you enjoy most?
- Did you work while attending high school?
- What were some of the jobs you had? Tell me what you took away from the experiences.
- What were your grades like?
- As a student, did you have to study hard or was course content something easily learned?

I move on to college, starting with, "How did you select the school you attended?" and then I repeat the process above, asking the same or similar questions I asked about high school. I finish with how they selected their major and what was the vision for their career when making the choice.

You might ask, "What does all this accomplish to uncover core values and core qualities?" We are looking for consistency. If the person received good grades for eight years of school, we can assume a certain level of intelligence or work ethic. Working while in school shows that someone understands the value of money early on. Consistently participating in sports or extracurricular activities displays commitment, teamwork, and the desire to be part of something beyond what is required. Why these choices were made speaks to the individual's overall thought process. Consistent high performance through school demonstrates a track record and speaks to our core quality of Drive. An example: If a candidate tells me he went to college because two friends were attending there, he did not work while attending school, and he graduated with a 2.8 GPA (but had a 3.8 GPA in his major), I can assume his overall drive is low. This person makes easy choices and will work hard only when he absolutely has to, if at all. Is it an exact science? No, but I will take the person who had consistent grades above a 3.25 GPA, consistently participated in activities, worked a job through school, and had a specific, career-related reason for choosing a college. Past behavior is the best predictor of future behavior. If people have the core qualities needed to succeed and share your core values to govern behavior, hard skills can be easily learned along the way. For Millennials this helps put some structure around the hiring process and some science to how we evaluate talent new to their career.

SHARE WECULTURE WITH POTENTIAL HIRES

If core values are so important to the success of the business, we should share what our core values are in the interview process. As WeCulture grew and I was promoted to the RVP role, we got creative and made Fatheads for the walls. We had apparel, wristbands, and signature pickers for emails. WeCulture was displayed proudly by all. While interviewing candidates, I would walk them over to the our WeCulture poster and show them what it was and explain our core values. I would tell them how we started WeCulture and give examples of how it drove actions to deliver results.

EVALUATING SKILLS AND ACCOMPLISHMENTS

Now that we have covered core values and core qualities, we can move on to skills and accomplishments. Screening for these two areas should be second nature to people in the staffing industry, frankly, because it is our everyday job. For other industries, there are various methods that can be used depending on the role.

Quantitative testing can be used where applicable and help give hiring managers tangible measure to evaluate a potential hire's skills. A good example would be testing an accountant on Microsoft Excel. If efficiency in Excel is a big part of the job, then using a testing product can give accurate insight on how a candidate will perform. Testing has a residual benefit. Many box products for skills testing offer overall scores, break down specific areas of expertise, and can offer rankings versus the population of those taking the same evaluation. With this information, if we are putting core values and core qualities before skills, we can now evaluate if teaching a skill is worth the investment. If you had the right individual who shares your core values, vision, and core qualities, is it worth it to teach them pivot tables in Excel? My experience in staffing shows that most hiring managers reject the candidate who came up short on Excel even if they had the right core values and qualities. We can teach Excel in a few short weeks; core value alignment and core qualities cannot be taught, and misalignment is the main cause of turnover, above hard skills.

Teach your team to use quantitative questions when measuring skills and accomplishments. If a candidate said she delivered a project ahead of schedule and under budget, my next questions are designed to measure that statement. What was the budget? What was the percentage saved? What was the deadline for the project? What was the final delivery date? What was the duration of the project? So the candidate told us she finished ahead of schedule and below budget? What if the savings was a hundred dollars on a million-dollar budget and three days on an eighteen-month timeline? Here quantification absolutely matters, and if we are asking questions to quantify, we can measure initial qualitative claims of success accurately.

Interview teams can be used to great effect with structure. Having a prep meeting prior to the interview to assign specific areas of technical skill or work history for each interviewer to cover based on his or her own skills is a recommended best practice. This will allow for a deep dive into specific skill areas and accomplishment. By the way, while we are evaluating skills, if your team is tuned in on core values and core qualities, everyone will be looking for signs of a good culture fit.

DEBRIEF FOR SUCCESS

Team debriefs should be done within twenty-four hours of the last interview. All team members should bring in notes from their time with a candidate and share open and honest feedback on what they learned. Qualitative and quantitative information should be shared. Again, for skills and accomplishments, this is easy. How can we quantify core values and core qualities? Below is a scorecard we used during interview debriefs. We set up a scoring system based on a scale of one to ten with a scorecard below.

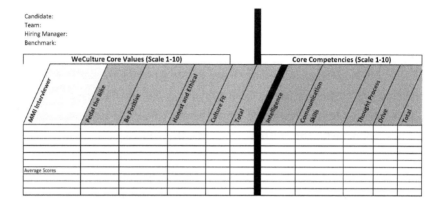

Each debrief will have a team lead to facilitate. Interviewers are asked to come to the meeting with ratings in each category using a current colleague as the base line for scoring. Having a baseline is critical because it adds an objective anchor to scoring. A score of ten in intelligence for one person can be an eight for another without a common point of comparison. The benchmark colleague should be someone similar to the individual we are evaluating. If you are interviewing a Millennial, then use a Millennial from your team. Comparing a Baby Boomer to a Millennial is an apples-and-oranges comparison. I would also use colleagues in similar roles whenever possible.

Below is a completed WeCulture Candidate Evaluation Scorecard.

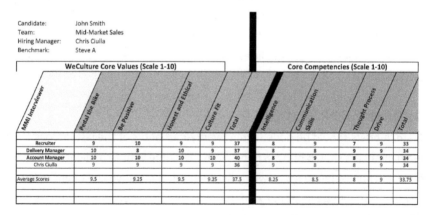

Scores are filled in and totaled by row, looking for average total scores for core values and core qualities for the applicant. For our scoring system, an average score of thirty-six or higher suggests a strong match for hire. With average scores of thirty-two to thirty-six, we will discuss and measure skills and accomplishments with greater weight. Anyone below a thirty is not a strong possibility of a good match. If they are not a match on core values and core qualities, the chance of turnover will be much higher. This goes back to the point already made several times: The main reason for turnover is related to culture fit. Skills match is rarely the reason for turnover. I believe this is because skills can be taught; core values and qualities cannot be taught. Taking this into account, a quantitative measure of core values and core qualities to evaluate hires should be worth the effort.

MEASURE YOUR OPPORTUNITY AGAINST THE CANDIDATE'S EXPECTATIONS

It is not just about employer expectations; candidates have expectations too. Like any relationship in life, if one party's expectations are not met, the relationship will come to an end. Millennials are now the majority of the workforce, having an average tenure of less than three years. Recent graduates will average three jobs in four years. How this new breed of employee is motivated is different than Generation X and the Baby Boomers. Money and individual achievement are second to meaningful work and being part of a greater purpose. Many interviewers are so focused on what candidates can do for the company or team that they rarely dig deep into what a candidate is looking for. WeCulture is about employee engagement, leveraging core values to grow the business. Some good questions for an interview to flush out a candidate's true expectations:

- What are your career expectations?
- What is the ideal work environment for you?
- How do you like to be led or managed?
- Forgetting this job, what is your dream job and why?
- What types of daily activities would make you look forward to coming into work tomorrow?

Questions like "Where do you see yourself in five years?" or "Why did you leave your last job?" only scratch the surface with regard to a candidate's vision for his or her own future.

Define expectation from each applicant and see how your role measures up. If your company has the potential to meet the expectations of the candidate, the chances of a successful hire, as well as long-term retention, increase. In staffing our job is nonstop interaction with external customers — both companies and candidates. Income is base salary plus commission on transactional sales, and all KPI's and results are for public display. In WeCulture the team comes first. If a Millennial wanted to deal with people, sell something meaningful to the customer, and be able to influence his or her own income while working on a team, then a job with our team in staffing should meet their expectations.

One of my most memorable hires was a candidate I almost decided not to call. Thank God I did. She was working for a retail paint store, and her job was selling paint to contractors. Most of her role was for large orders, and the target audience was quite different from IT staffing. We diligently followed our interview process and discovered her scores were thirty-seven for core values and thirty-six for core qualities. On top of this, she was leaving her current role to deal with a more professional client base and wanted to sell something that would add unique value to the end customer. She knew nothing about staffing or IT; her skills match was nonexistent. We hired her anyway, and after three months, she was making placements and finding people jobs. By her second year, she was one of my region's most consistent recruiters, earning the #1 or #2 slot every month ahead of staff with more than double her tenure. She loved coming to work every day, and it showed. This individual was successful because she shared our core values and had the desired core qualities. The job exceeded her personal expectations, giving us the best possible match.

Make sure "we" includes the people you hire too.

LEVERAGE THE HIRING PROCESS TO BUILD TRUST

While companies are determined to hire top talent and improve the process, candidates have a bit of a different perspective. We all read online and through LinkedIn posts about job seekers frustrations with the hiring process. There are posts by employment experts about challenges with talent acquisition, online portals being impersonal/outdated/cumbersome, no feedback or generic replies to applications, poor interview experiences, outdated tactics to evaluate talent, and long periods of silence or missed opportunities for communication. The most-talented candidates have options, and a poor first impression will send them looking for the next great opportunity with your competitor.

Knowing these are the challenges, how can organizations and hiring managers change to attract top talent? While we cannot influence supply-and-demand factors for qualified candidates, companies can focus on what they can control by adapting hiring practices to attract and engage potential applicants. Below are some suggestions that can help and require an introspective look. The good news is it can be done with little or no cost.

Overcommunicate

Once you engage a candidate, communicate with them like a potential valued partner. This can be as simple as offering choices on interview times (phone, onsite, Skype) that account for a working candidate's commitments to their current employer. Possibly talk by phone whenever possible for setting next steps, requesting information, talking through onboarding process, and benefits review. Candidates do place a very high value on phone and face-to-face interaction, which helps build the bond between the hiring company's colleagues and the applicant. Building this relationship on the front end with care will ensure a better chance an offer is accepted and increase retention. If a candidate is disqualified for the role, the recruiter or manager who interviewed them should make a phone call and share why. Any impression you leave could be shared on social media and could help or hurt the company image.

Share Your Hiring Process Start to Finish

This should be done when you invite a candidate in for the first phone interview. Very common critical feedback from candidates regarding the interview process is that they have no idea what the next steps are or where the finish line is. Silence can derail any positive impression built and leave the best candidates looking at other opportunities while waiting. More often than not, this is unintentional, and busy hiring managers can help themselves by setting expectations for next steps in the process. If you like a candidate, set the next step in the interview process. This can be a simple as setting a follow-up call with a calendar invite, and it will build trust with the applicant. Keep in mind, once a candidate is committed to leaving his or her current employer, the best of the best will want to create options. Maybe this person had no desire to leave a current employer until you called them, but now that he or she has made the choice to move on, he or she could start taking recruiter calls that were ignored in the past. A slow process opens the door for other employers to step in and leave you competing for the best talent.

Make a Plan and Stick to It

So now that you have done a great job communicating intentions and outlined a great process, it is time for the hiring team to execute. Nothing builds trust and a long-lasting relationship more than doing what you say you will do, and hiring is no different. If you were dating someone, and he or she routinely rescheduled/cancelled dates, missed calls, or put other priorities first, anyone who is that perfect person would probably end the relationship. Hiring is no different, and cancelling an interview says to great candidates that they are not a priority. While your company sends this message, the competition for your potential next star colleagues might steal them away. The hiring process is the beginning of a relationship that all parties hope will be mutually beneficial. A tip for leaders hiring by committee: treat hiring like any other project you manage — set a goal, define the right candidate before you post the job, set a budget, set a process (including who they will meet), and agree with your team to a target offer and acceptance date. Work your interview process backward from there and have all members commit to interview times in advance. (Don't worry — if you can't find a candidate to fill an interview slot, team members will be grateful to have their time back.)

An Unexpected Final Handshake

As a hiring manager, you can't say no to your unpredictable boss, right? What a savvy hiring manager can do is approach the C-level leader before the team kickoff meeting and invite them to join in. If they say yes, now you are making them part of the normal process. Socialize this step to applicants. Trust me, managing multiple locations for years, I always appreciated being invited to the interview process for field staff early on, and if I felt I needed to see a hire after the "final," nothing would stop me from meeting them.

Candidates expecting offers who get an invite back for another unscheduled round see this as a delay at best; at worst it impacts their opinions of their new potential leaders. Indecisive? Does this new person insert themselves on a whim for everything or just hires? So many applicants blow it for this meeting, and recruiters set them up for failure, telling them, "Oh they just want to shake hands." In reality C-level executives are smart and great at evaluating talent (that is how they became executives). It is an interview for sure, and if it does not get taken seriously by the candidate, that handshake is to say good-bye to a job offer.

Deliver Offers on Time and at the Terms Discussed in the Interview

In larger companies, offer letters can take time to get. As long as you set the time-line, a great candidate will be patient. After all the hard work to get to the finish line, let's not break the trust with a delay. I have also personally been the victim of working for a leader trying to save a buck with low-ball offers. My last boss was always haggling for less on the offer letter at the end of the process. Maybe we save a small amount now, but even if the candidate accepts the offer, calls continue to come his or her way with opportunities. Your new hires may feel slighted and leave if someone gives them the extra money. This goes back to doing what you say you will do to build trust. Low-ball offers are a relationship killer and are sure to mar your relationship with a new employee. The best candidates often walk away, and even if you come back with their agreed terms, they could reject the offer.

Take a look at your last three hires. Ask your hiring team what kind of impression the hiring process makes on applicants. What can you change? If you do a great job communicating with top talent, provide a positive experience during interviews, follow a defined hiring process, and deliver a timely offer at the agreed terms, you will be leveraging your hiring process to attract the best of the best.

We have spent a considerable amount of time discussing and reviewing hiring. The foundation of any successful business is built with the right people. Identifying, screening and attracting the best talent takes discipline and a consistent process. If you are committed to long-lasting success for the organization and those you are charged to lead, put WeCulture's approach into practice. Hire great people for the right reasons and partner with them to achieve great results.

Now that we have the right people, it is time to get them to execute!

"Strategy without tactics is the slowest path to victory; tactics without strategy is the noise before defeat."

— *Sun Tzu, ancient Chinese military strategist*

CHAPTER SEVEN
OPERATIONAL EFFECTIVENESS

The right talent is the foundation of any great organization. The framework we build upon it is based on standard operating procedures (SOP's) to get the right people working toward the same goals. The definition of standard operating procedures — these are written instructions intended to document how to perform a routine activity to help ensure consistency and quality of products or services. While a chapter on SOP's does not sound exciting, they are also a critical part of leveraging WeCulture to drive results. Standard operating procedures are not just for the back-office functions or manufacturing floor. Every team, every department, every employee should be guided on consistent methodology. How can standard operating procedures contribute to driving corporate culture?

One of WeCulture's tenets we used while building our business was focused on teamwork. "The best teams make better players." I made this part of WeCulture because of what was outlined in chapter six: hire people who share your core values and core qualities first. These are players with potential to be great who need a forum to nurture their talents. The only way a team can make better players is through professional skills development. How are skills developed? In the book *Grit* by Angela Duckworth, the point is made regarding talent being a myth. Talent = success. We look at highly successful people, and talent becomes the excuse, a reason not to compete. To dispel the myth, the point is made that talent alone cannot bring results. The true formula is:

- Talent x <u>effort</u> = skill
- Skill x <u>effort</u> = achievement

Talent can be applied through effort, and repeating a process consistently over time will develop skill. Apply effort to a well-honed skill, and we have achievement. Take professional athletes as an example of how talent is developed into a skill. The best athletes spend countless hours executing repeatable processes to make how they play second nature. They not only practice for hours — they practice specific techniques for hours. They focus on a standard way to execute. In *Grit* the author talks about the ten-thousand-hour rule — the average number of hours it takes to become an expert at applying specific skills. J.J. Watt, defensive end for the Houston Texans, is one of the best defensive players in the NFL, and to achieve success, he spent most of his life playing the game. His achievements include multiple Pro Bowl selections, and he has been ranked in the top five for defensive players in the NFL three of the last four years. As an NFL player, every aspect of practice, conditioning, and diet are carefully scripted and followed to keep up peak performance. His raw talent could never achieve this level of success without consistent training, careful study of the playbook, watching hours of game film on the competition, and execution of specific techniques. He has talent, but his success comes through consistently executing a plan based on standard procedures. Imagine if J.J. Watt did not execute any of the carefully planned procedures in his routine. Let's say he did not follow his specific diet and gained weight. If Watt were out of shape, he would move slower, and in the NFL, even one-tenth of a second can change the outcome of a play.

Now back to how this applies in the business world. Sales professionals are viewed as athletes in organizations. Executives often describe top producing sales reps as "rock stars," "rainmakers," or overachievers who have that undefinable "it" — qualities we all wish we could bottle and give to the rest of the team to realize the same level of results. I'm a born-bred, bonus-fed salesperson. I grew up selling and in staffing won several awards for top-level production, including rookie of the year when I joined the staffing industry. If only I could attribute this success to some myth based on my level of talent, my life as a sales professional would have been so much easier. I have no undefinable "it," no secret sauce. I am unremarkable in almost every way — a slightly overweight, Italian guy from Staten Island. When people look at me, they don't say, "I can see why people buy from him." As a son of a fireman, I had no inside track to the business world. I'm not athletic, not overly handsome, not super smart, and went to a city college. When I look back at how I achieved success in sales, it was because of execution. It was exceeding the standard operating procedures for sales activity every week. The goal was a hundred connecting phone calls and ten client meetings, I just out-dialed others, which led to more connecting calls to client contacts, helping me average fifteen meetings a week. We believed in role-playing and did it every week. Even after I was top ten worldwide, we still role-played every week. I still exceeded my call and visit volume every week. I take job orders from clients following a standard process taught to me as a rookie to this day. I manage client hiring processes using the techniques executed since 1998 to help guide clients and candidates. As I partner with the sales teams I am charged to lead, I teach these techniques to them, and there is accountability to execute — standard operating procedures for sales to bring consistent results.

My first manager was big on execution. He was a college football player for Notre Dame coached by the legend Lou Holtz and part of the national championship team in 1988. His belief was that talent comes to the surface through discipline. In his mind, business was no different than football — the best teams build better players. A leader's job is to outline what it takes to succeed and hold the team accountable to follow the plays.

Now that we have established the importance execution and how standard operating procedures can drive individual success, how does this fit in with WeCulture? In any work environment, individuals are dependent on other team members, departments, or managers to support their efforts. Maybe when a business is small, an owner can touch each desk and drive actions. As success is achieved and the business grows, colleagues must know what is expected and be able to execute their parts without direction. Standard operating procedures will define performance of individuals and contribute to the overall operational effectiveness of any organization. WeCulture is based on engaging employees by creating a positive work environment. The core value of Pedal the Bike is based on effort but also defines and measures KPI's that truly drive results with a focus on the team meeting goals. If everyone is executing according to a well-designed plan that has easy-to-follow procedures, we can build trust throughout the organization. Think about it: If we can feel confident that our colleagues we depend on to win will have processes to govern action along with core values, we can spend time on our own activities to drive results. It is easy to focus on execution of your own job when you can count on those around you. In sales our job is to close the deal. New customer or existing customer, good sales professionals bring the business in and then leave it to the operational teams to deliver the product or service to the client. I know firsthand selling for years that this requires an extraordinary amount of trust. WeCulture's Core Value #3 is Honest and Ethical. Teams function effectively and achieve goals when individuals can trust the person sitting next to them to do his or her job.

I was charged as a sales professional in staffing to get clients to hire from our company. Back at our office, there was a team of recruiters that identified candidates for open requirements. These recruiters depended on me to bring in jobs to give their time spent on qualifying candidates value. Without their hard work, I would have no "product" to sell to clients. We count on each other to execute for the office to make placements. This can be applied to any industry. It's pretty hard to keep a client in a manufacturing sale when the shipping department always ships orders late. If the billing department does not invoice clients properly, it does not matter how much product we sell, clients won't pay. If accounts payable does not process payment for raw materials or pay utility bills on time, it can bring the business to a grinding halt. What is in place so that each of these departments can know how and when to do each of these critical business functions? Standard operating procedures.

Every job big or small becomes important, and the little details can add up for or against the business. Like key performance indicators, SOP's must be written so that they guide the team toward efficient, meaningful activity. What gives activity meaning as it relates to standard operating procedures? Good standard operating procedures should tie back to two things: tasks that grow the business and tasks that protect the business from risk. As we made WeCulture part of our organization, we not only focused on what needed to be done, but we focused on why we needed to do it, along with who would be responsible to execute on the team. Why we were asked to execute and who would be responsible on the team were just as critical as what the procedure actually was. Once colleagues understood why and we tied it back to how the procedure helps the team, getting people to execute was easy. Remember, a key motivator for Millennials is the "why" behind what they do, along with how their jobs contribute to the big picture. Meaningful work contributes to effort and retention. We can use SOP's as a means to engage colleagues by being transparent about how their work impacts the business. Forget Millennials — give work meaning for any colleague from any generation, and you will have a more engaged workforce.

For sales we followed some simple guidelines to define responsibilities early on. While we were building the office and developing our WeCulture, it took time for the sales professionals to trust the organization to deliver. We held a meeting with all colleagues to help clarify roles and responsibilities. The team took all tasks done at every desk from the beginning of the sales cycle through a successful placement (meaning assignment completed with a client satisfied) and categorized these activities into two categories: presale and postsale activities. Presale activities would be everything done to win the sale right up to the candidate start date. Postsales would include all services and tasks related to the placement after the start date. As we listed out each task, we then started to write the title of the position on our organizational chart to define who was responsible for this task. During this part of the exercise, there was a considerable amount of debate, but once we finished the exercise, every task had been assigned, and this became the foundation of procedures we followed to service our clients. Remember, in chapter two we described this office: no communication among colleagues, poor execution, dismal results. The reality was grounded in core values, but the layer deeper was that standard operating procedures for many tasks were defined but not assigned. Without assignment to specific team members, many critical tasks that were part of standard operating procedure often fell through the cracks. The failure to execute was the fault of leadership. An example: Sales would assume references were done by recruiters on placed candidates, and recruiters would expect the sales team to make these calls. The result was these calls were not made. Once we assigned this role to our recruiters, we were 100 percent compliant for references on all placements in future audits. For this company, documented procedure was not enough. Once references were assigned and there was clear instruction on who was accountable, the work was done consistently. Consistent execution allowed the sales people to trust that this task was done, and now they could focus more time on developing new sales.

For business owners, this can be a critical exercise and is something I recommend at times when the organization faces growing pains. Growing pains in businesses can be a result of process gaps, being short staffed, or failure to execute. In WeCulture the organization is free from blame because the leader is ultimately responsible for the actions and behavior of those they are charged to lead. Next time you discover a repeating gap in services, host a meeting with the colleagues involved and ask them to list out the procedure related to the point of failure. In this meeting, take a seat as an observer and appoint a colleague to facilitate. Can the team define the process? Based on what is required, are resources available to efficiently and effectively complete the task? Can the team agree on who is responsible for each task to achieve the goal? Are the people responsible trained and capable? There will likely be gaps uncovered through the exercise. Moments of discomfort. You may have colleagues who you thought were executing and find out they were not. Remember, this is not a time to focus on past behavior or negative feelings associated with the catalyst for the meeting. The goal is work as a team, define a process, and move forward with a plan to succeed next time. We will talk more about effective meetings for WeCulture later in the book.

Standard operating procedures can change over time to meet the needs of the business. This is a critical thing to note and something missed in many organizations. More often than not, outdated procedures will remain on the books. Those executing will say things like, "But this is how we have always done this." Other obstacles can be the time and investment to making needed changes or the most common: the unconscious resistance to change that everyone has. A key difference between core values and standard operating procedures is that core values are timeless and never changing. Standard operating procedures must change and are the company's means of adapting to the ever-changing world around it.

When we launched WeCulture, the business grew exponentially, and as we were bringing in new clients, there was a risk uncovered for the near future. Many of our new clients were requiring our company to hold the W-2 of the contractors we employed. This presented several unique challenges for our business because our recruiting efforts were very dependent on supply-chain partners to identify talent, and our company had no formal process to hold H-1B or TN visas. In technology staffing, a very large percentage of the workforce is represented by foreign-born nationals requiring sponsorship to be employed in the U.S. Why? Next time you are at a cocktail party with friends or family, ask all the people who have children how many are encouraging their kids to be developers? You won't see many hands go up, yet the backbone of almost everything we do depends on people employed to write code. Your smartphone's applications, everything we see or do on the Internet, every appliance, every car — and almost every product we use — is made with machines. All these machines are hardware that operates driven by lines of code.

As we identified this challenge, WeCulture kicked in immediately. One of our tenets posted on the wall is "Always be solutions-focused." We brainstormed our ideas based on competitive intelligence gathered to come up with our own visa-transfer program. This would give us a standard operating procedure to attract and retain technology professionals who required sponsorship to work on our W-2. Coming up with a plan was the easy part. The real challenge was that we were part of a publicly traded company and had to convince it that the procedures needed to be changed. Our focus was on why and the benefit to clients, candidates, and our organization. If we reduced dependencies on supply-chain partners and candidates could be paid a bit more, clients would get a better price, and we would get higher margins. We were taking the money saved that was normally paid to a supply-chain partner to cover the legal cost of sponsorship and split the saving among all three parties to achieve mutually assured value.

Standard operating procedures define how we will execute. Provided these SOP's are designed to drive sales, mitigate risk, and serve the client, adherence should drive desired results. As colleagues can count on others, trust will follow. Think about how this applies to almost every aspect of daily life. When you see a green light at an intersection, you drive through it because you trust that other drivers (complete strangers) will stop for a red light. I take the train to work twice a week. Because I can count on the transit system to be on time, I can build how I execute my own day without a second thought. Within organizations we need the same level of trust to build good culture. Who do you bring to work every day? When you perform your job, do you focus on the task or how this task contributes to the larger goal? How can you tie in your responsibilities to the success of the teams around you? This is how we build culture. This is how routine tasks have meaning — how little things add up to create good culture. You don't have to be a manager to drive culture. Who creates the culture? We all do through our actions and behaviors — actions and behaviors governed by simple core values and now the steps on how to execute defined through standard operating procedures.

This becomes the playbook for everyone to Pedal the Bike in the same direction; the rally point to focus Be Positive, making "we can" a reality; an Honest and Ethical look at individual and team performance with a defined basis point.

There are four critical aspects to leverage standard operating procedures to build good culture. First is "Followed By All." We cannot have exceptions or allow for colleagues to consistently violate procedures in place. Mistakes will happen, and it is our responsibility to help other colleagues when honest errors are made. There are times when people will not execute or knowingly bypass procedures. This could be a manager who leads with a "do as I say, not as I do" approach or a top sales producer who does not properly post sales for revenue recognition to avoid administrative work. Maybe you made a hiring mistake, and the person in the chair just does not live up to WeCulture core values. Regardless, willful failure to execute is yet another form of culture cancer that cannot be ignored. Let colleagues knowingly violate procedures, and you put the enterprise at risk. Also your best colleagues will be saddled with the extra work this failure creates. Over the long haul, this can create the worst kind of turnover — the best people doing all the extra work will get frustrated and eventually leave. The rule is simple: bad people = bad things. Keep them around long enough, and there is a good chance that something bad will happen to you.

The second critical element is training. Remember my first boss in staffing? His method to ensure proper execution was consistent training on standards of execution. This included his back-office team and our administrative staff. You will play exactly how you practice. Take training seriously, and so will those you are charged to lead. One of our tenets is "Better teams make better players." Training is a partnership between the company and the colleagues at all levels, regardless of tenure. The company has an obligation to deliver continuous training. The market will change all around us; complacency will only lead to failure. While the company has a responsibility to deliver training, the burden of learning is the colleague's. Here Pedal the Bike is a critical value, and even when we train, giving 100 percent is expected at all times. Pro athletes practice and train every day, and if they don't take the drills seriously, performance, when it counts, will fail. As people practice a technique to develop a skill, this can spur innovation. The best players are always pushing the limits. With WeCulture's focus on the team, this innovation can be shared, documented, and become standard operating procedures.

Involve your existing staff in training new hires. This will not only help new colleagues learn but will also continually reinforce standard operating procedures with existing staff. A residual benefit will be bonding among peers while spending time together. Often senior staff will take pride in the success of new hires if they participate in the training process. If you are launching a new product, new system, or any new procedure, send a staff-level colleague to be trained and have them facilitate the training back to the group. This will create "power users" in the department and help your high-potential staff develop leadership skills for the future. Those learning a new skill will appreciate the extra work done by others to provide training and build respect among the team.

Third, everyone has their part to play. Standard operating procedures define how we do things and help us deliver a consistent product or service. "Who" is just as important as "how" we do things and "what" is actually done. Ultimately someone must be accountable to complete tasks or ensure critical functions are covered. If everyone is responsible, then no one is. Make sure each procedure refers back to the title or position in the organization responsible so that everyone on the team understands their roles in how we achieve success. A good example: I volunteer for a theater group twice a year building sets and props. Imagine a theater production in action during a show. The backstage crew all know the play inside and out and what scenery goes where and when. The areas we work in are dark and tight for space, and timing means everything. If we have specific people assigned to each piece of equipment, props, or scenery, we can then coordinate movement, placement, and timing as a team. If we did not focus on who performs each task, it would be chaos backstage. Some pieces would be moved; others could sit idle while backstage crew members assume someone else would do it. We would compromise safety, moving large, heavy pieces in an uncoordinated effort. Believe it or not, backstage is an injury-prone environment even when we are completely focused on execution. Knowing who is responsible matters and will increase efficiency while building trust in the process.

Lastly, document all standard operating procedures. For publicly traded companies, this is a must under the Sarbanes Oxley Act, but for smaller, privately held companies, this is often a gap that can hinder performance. It also creates a greater risk when there is turnover because no one will know exactly how things get done. A good example is with sales professionals. Often the battle rages between management and sales regarding documentation in the CRM system. The risk is if the salesperson leaves anything not documented in the system, it all leaves with them. Target clients are not realized, and historical data on prospects is lost. In staffing sales, people would save documents in Excel or Outlook. One of my first projects was to create a master list of all signed client contracts. Salespeople would get them signed and stick them in a desk drawer, laptop hard drive, or personal Outlook folder. This was done in the office I took over for years before I arrived even though the SOP was to house all contracts in the corporate shared drive. Once the sale professional left the company, these contracts would get lost, and we would have no record of business terms agreed to with a client. To avoid the risk of lost contracts related to turnover, we documented the procedure, made it part of training, and required a countersigned client agreement filed on the shared drive to get paid commissions on each sale.

We have made some meaningful progress so far with WeCulture. We established who is responsible to create the culture, defined core values to guide behavior, developed a method to identify, attract, and hire the right talent, and described a way to leverage standard operating procedures, building trust through execution. To this point, WeCulture is a universal methodology and thought process that can be applied to any business. How do we customize WeCulture for your business? It is time to look at specific goals, industry drivers, and the needs of your business. In chapter eight, we will define tenets for WeCulture to tie in all the things that are specific to your organization's success.

"Be sure you put your feet in the right place, then stand firm."

— Abraham Lincoln

CHAPTER EIGHT
TENETS TO GUIDE YOUR VISION

While we look at the core values associated with WeCulture to guide our vision, organizations can keep their unique identities by building tenets. In chapter six, we talked about hiring using WeCulture core values to benchmark candidates, combined with core qualities. Core qualities are what we use to customize the WeCulture hiring process to match up to the company's specific needs. Tenets will provide the same effect on a larger scale, helping reinforce adoption of WeCulture, including specifics on how it fits the needs of the business. A tenet is defined as a principle or belief. For business we can leverage a principle to reinforce core values, digging deeper to drive behavior customized to our business. I was in the staffing business. Therefore when we created our tenets for WeCulture, they were specifically designed for our environment. In this chapter, we will share each one, discuss how it ties back to WeCulture core values, and share examples for other industries, provided it is relevant.

On the following page is a sample WeCulture Fathead similar to the one displayed in the common areas for every office in our region.

The definition of selling: (from the dictionary) To be employed to persuade or induce others to buy.

Our CRM/ATS is the only system of record for the region including standardized documentation methodology.

Selling is defined by our ability to influence the outcome and will always require the BDM and the RDM working as a team.

Better teams make better players. They have people who care about the success of the business and work together.

Sales is a full contact sport. We set ourselves up to win by making regular contact with our clients/candidates. KPI FOCUS.

Live the company core values.

Our goal is to have every colleague make more money than last year

Sales is a competitive game and requires that we give 100% to win. Judge performance based on results and effort.

Professional Development is part of every 1 on 1

Hire diverse teams focused on core qualities; intelligence, communication skills, thought process, and DRIVE.

Always be solutions focused to help the client and candidate. Make their satisfaction our primary goal.

As you can see, the tenets are clearly listed, along with the image of WeCulture core values. Defining tenets can be done in a similar fashion to how you define core qualities for hiring. My recommendation is to set a meeting with department leaders only and invite key colleagues at the staff level to help. The group should be about seven to ten people. Ask each person to make a list of specific beliefs or principles they would use to help drive the business. After lists are made, cross-reference each one and circle anything listed two or more times. Anything listed once should be discussed by the team and then items listed twice and so on until each item listed is discussed. Anything the group agrees should not be there because it cannot be tied into core values should be erased. Use the remaining items and have open discussion with a target to narrow this list down to the seven to ten tenets you believe match for your business. To guide the discussion, you can use the below questions.

- How does this tenet tie back to core values?
- Will this principle guide behavior in a positive way?
- Does this help promote teamwork?
- Can this belief be applied to all colleagues?
- How will this help us achieve our goals?
- Does this fit with our business?

We were a staffing company set up in a field-office structure with 90 percent of all field staff in some capacity of sales or recruiting. Even sales and recruiting leaders sold in some capacity, which makes our tenets focus primarily on teamwork and results. Let's take a look at how tenets were defined and applied as we rebuild the business discussed in chapter two.

1. ***"The definition of selling (from the dictionary): To be employed to persuade or induce others to buy"***

   For our team, it was critical that we actually define what selling is. Many of our hires were new to their careers (Millennials), and more than half of our colleagues were recruiters. Many of the recruiters would often say, "I'm not in sales," yet nothing could be further from the truth. Our sales staff sold our services and candidates to clients. Recruiters also sold on every call; they were selling jobs to candidates. Even though our service is free to candidates, we are still selling to them and providing a service. This makes every candidate a customer. I felt strongly that this should not only be a tenet for us, but it should also be the first. It set the tone that we are a sales organization. This ties back to our core value of Pedal the Bike, supporting the message of that core value to focus our energy on activities that matter.

   Another reason I felt this was important was that many salespeople say, "My client does not like to be sold to." For me this is a sentence fragment. The reality is your client does not want to be sold to by a salesperson who cannot add value. In staffing the primary skill is the ability to sell and display value for the customer, including the hiring managers and the candidates. Personally I love being sold to when the salesperson understands what I want, along with how their product of service adds value to satisfy the need. I buy preowned cars — usually lease returns with low miles and less than three years old. Once I decide what I am looking for, which will include a specific brand, make, and model, the hunt is on. My last purchase was a Ford F-150. I wanted the crew cab. I had three color choices. I wanted a FX4 or Lariat. I lined up a few dealerships over a few days and set out to have one by the end of the week. The first dealership I visited had the exact truck I was looking for, right down to specific options. It was my first color choice, had eighteen thousand miles, and was in perfect condition. The price was fair, and I did not feel the need to haggle. Seems easy and pretty lucky, right? After the test drive, the salesperson disappeared for about thirty minutes and returned with the sales manager, pressuring me to buy the truck. It was all hard sell — no value and nothing pleasant about him. After all, they had someone in an hour before me who was ready to put down a deposit, but I could beat that customer to it if I decided to buy it now. After fifteen minutes, I let them know I would think about it and left. Had the sales experience been focused on value, I would have bought the truck and drove it home. Two days later (on a Monday), I got a call from another dealership, one I never had heard of. The salesperson said I looked at their inventory online and asked me lots of questions about what I was looking for. We spent about thirty minutes on the phone, and after he felt we were on the same page, he directed me to the website and showed me six trucks that met my criteria that they had in stock. We set an appointment for me to visit; I left work early and took a trip about an hour away. This dealership was in the worst neighborhood I had ever seen and was not branded by Ford. I almost decided to drive past it, but then I saw all six trucks right out front, so I pulled in. The salesperson came out and greeted me immediately and said he knew it was me because he looked up my LinkedIn profile picture. We looked at all six trucks, and I test drove three. The place was busy, and there were customers with every salesperson on a Monday afternoon. I picked one and was ready to buy it. The sales manager, Freddy, greeted me with a smile, and after we quickly agreed to a price, he said, "Chris, we will detail the truck and have you out in two hours." I drove it home. I pulled into the lot at 3:30 and was driving home by 6. Why did I buy from these guys? From the minute the salesperson called me to the minute I left, they were selling. They took the time to learn about me, what I wanted, and then presented a product that met my criteria. I bought from this dealership because the sales team added value through the experience. I felt like their only customer even though they closed on eight cars while I was sitting there. Everyone likes to be sold to by good salespeople.

This tenet speaks to me and is a reminder to the team that our business is sales.

2. *"Selling is defined by our ability to influence the outcome and will always require the BDM and the RDM working as a team."*
Note: BDM is short for business development manager (salesperson), and RDM is resource development manager (recruiter).

Here we are exclusively focused on teamwork through execution of the company processes. As we reviewed in chapter seven, a big part of getting WeCulture to take hold is based on all staff following standard operating procedures. This tenet is directly connected to the core values of Be Positive and Honest and Ethical. Positive energy is reinforced through trust. Trust is fostered when colleagues can count on everyone to execute consistently as a team. The sales processes referenced in the tenet were focused on how we partnered with our customers to manage the hiring and how we dealt with business issues working together.

For us execution was critical to success. Our product is also a customer, and mistakes we make can impact careers. Having multiple colleagues involved to monitor the wants and needs of a client measured next to a candidate is a tricky business. We are not manufacturing brake pads, and machines are not calibrated to deliver to precise specifications — every deal is unique. If recruiters can communicate effectively with sales about a candidate's expectations, then we can measure this against what our clients have to offer. Salespeople will take job orders from customers, and miscommunications or missteps can often mar the deal. Why do I love the staffing business? If we work together communicating effectively as a team, a great candidate gets a better job.

Think about how this can apply to the food-service industry. I spent years doing front-of-house management, and there are many customers who want their order their way. A good waiter always asks how a steak should be prepared, and then it is up to the kitchen team to deliver. If a client orders a steak medium rare and the waiter delivers it well done, the dining experience is ruined. Not only does the kitchen staff have to prepare the steak medium rare, but they must also coordinate with wait staff to make sure the entree is delivered immediately. Too much time under a warming lamp and a warm, red center will start to turn gray.☺

3. *"Sales is a full-contact sport. We set ourselves up to win by making regular contact with our clients/candidates. KPI FOCUS."*

Seems pretty straightforward. Once we defined the KPI's that mattered, it became important that we have a reminder posted as a tenet of WeCulture. Clearly this speaks to the core value of Pedal the Bike and that winning and maintaining clients takes more than one call. For our business, company contacts were almost always repeat buyers. Therefore, part of our sales effort was client retention. Candidates did not jump at the first job we offered by phone, and the relationship with a recruiter is based on trust. We have made the point a few times already that changing jobs has a big impact on someone's life. Like us our candidate target audience knows this as well, and many will make career choices carefully.

One of my largest clients was early in my career. I was pursuing a client who was building a shared-services center in the heart of our sales territory, creating several hundred new jobs. I began calling in to the new leadership team and kept getting funneled to their corporate controller, so I started a regiment of regular calls and emails to him in an effort to win a client meeting. (Keep in mind this was before LinkedIn and other social media.) Weeks of calls, literature drops, and emailing resumes of available candidates were ignored. For most calls, if he picked up his line, he would hang up after I introduced myself. Finally after several weeks of calls, he said, "Chris, what do I have to do to get you to stop calling me!?!?!" My answer was, "Give me a shot on your next hire." So he did. As we wrapped up the call, he gave me the number and email address of one of his managers hiring two staff accountants. "Chris, if you fill the jobs, I would appreciate it if you don't contact me again."

I called the manager, and she was expecting my call — we filled both jobs in two weeks. As she was satisfied with the candidates, I kept in contact with her and both of them — regular visits, a welcome lunch, and I stocked both candidates' desks with our logo gear (mugs, post notes, staplers, pens, mouse pads, etc.) A few weeks later three of that manager's peers began working with me, and now we had twelve consultants billing. I repeated the same process with these new contacts, and candidates and referral continued. After a few months, we had over thirty consultants on billing. Regular contact to build out the business was almost easy. Sales is a full-contact sport, and the reality is it takes ten or more attempts to get a contact to say yes. It goes without saying the tenet meets the criteria to support WeCulture core values and drive results.

4.   *"Sales is a competitive game and requires that we give 100% to win. Judge performance based on results and effort."*

This was important to our colleagues at the time. The company we worked for was a pretty political organization, and we wanted a principle focused on objective performance measures. Effort can be measured through KPI's, and performance could be tied to financial results for each business unit. No favorites in WeCulture — just Core Values that drive desired behavior and results. Our company was primarily a sales environment with lots of type A personalities. The number-one reason people buy is because they like the salesperson. Since many of us in sales leadership are wired to count on subjective factors to win business, it is only natural that subjective measures can cloud judgement when it comes to performance. KPI's and results versus the business plan give us objective measures to guide how we evaluate progress. As we take an objective approach, first it brings science to performance management. We can then consider circumstances and soft skills to factor in subjective measures. Performance management is art and science, and if we use objective measures first, we can weigh subjective measures to see if it reinforces our clinical view.

An example would be a sales colleague on our team who is below plan 40 percent YTD versus financial results. Client meetings were eight versus a goal of ten the past four weeks, and the sales funnel for future opportunities is light. Sounds like someone who is not Pedaling the Bike. Objective measures would say this colleague is an underperformer. We look to add in circumstances, and as a company, we had decided to walk away from her largest client due to a new contract with unfavorable business terms, which had been her exclusive focus. Her consulting portfolio grinded to a halt, and she had to start over hunting for new clients. My thoughts here with her managing director were to overlook financial results and judge performance for the next ninety days based on KPI's while we helped her on sales calls to secure new business.

A second example would be a colleague with us six months at 60 percent of the financial plan. As we look at KPI's, the person is also at 50 to 60 percent of expectations each week. We factored in that other new hires were meeting performance for KPI's and results. Was this colleague an underperformer? Absolutely. As we used objective measures, we were also supporting our core values based on being Honest and Ethical. We had standards to measure performance and, provided there was transparency, the team would understand if a colleague was terminated. If the team shared our core values, asking people to leave that did not display our core values through their behavior would be seen as something positive.

5. *"Always be solutions-focused to help the client and candidate. Make their satisfaction our primary goal."*
WeCulture depends on teamwork, and in order to work as a team, we need a common goal. Putting the client first is a great way to find common ground, especially in a tough situation. In staffing, recruiters and sales professionals have a codependent relationship — one group cannot succeed without the other. When things go wrong, this tenet becomes critical to problem-solving. Too many times coworkers and leaders are focused on what went wrong, how it happened, and who is responsible before we even solve the problem at hand. In simple terms, "blame" can take center stage, and once it does, colleagues who can help you solve the problem will tune out. We cannot stress enough that blame is a form of culture cancer. If we put how/what/who of the problem ahead of the work to resolve the issue at hand, the client will come second. The residual long-term consequences can condition colleagues to hide a small challenge or hold back critical information. If we put the client first above all else, we can engage colleagues on working toward a solution as a team with a common goal. Keep in mind, while we put the client first, once the issue is solved, we can do a debrief. After we satisfy the client, we can usually look at the cause of the problem, and cooler heads will prevail. If

someone made a mistake, it can become a coaching moment. We can also clinically look at our own procedures and thought processes, performing gap analysis to prevent the situation in the future. When things go wrong, it can create pressure where the team must act quickly. This pressure can be a positive influence, provided we keep our collective energy on the client first. For Millennials a primary motivator is to be part of the big picture, working toward the greater good. Solving a problem through a difficult situation can build lasting bonds, and good leaders will use this as a means to foster employee engagement. This tenet reinforces WeCulture's core value Be Positive.

6. *"Our CRM/ATS is the only system of record for the region including standardized documentation methodology."*
    Common usage of a CRM or ATS tool to support WeCulture? This is not a stretch. Promoting standards for how we use systems builds trust and supports WeCulture Core Value #3 Honest and Ethical. Almost everything we do in the corporate world is dependent on technology and documented using a technology tool; staffing was not different. With hundreds of open requirements and thousands of candidates in the market, all being called by a staff of over sixty colleagues, we needed technology to help us manage the process. Think about this: If a recruiter calls a candidate for a job opportunity, how would any other recruiter also working the job know that candidate was called — aside from lost time through duplication of effort? What does this say to the candidate about our company? If salespeople from the same office are calling the same client contacts, what impression will we make? Does this help us or hurt us as we pursue business?

    Failure to document in the system can create trust issues and conflict. A good example is when a client gives us a requirement to work on, and two sales professionals claim the sale. Both called the contact without the other knowing, and now both expect to be paid. If there is no documentation in the system, figuring this out can be difficult. The manager can listen to the situation and decide — or call the client to figure it out in rare instances. Multiply this time and effort by fifty-plus open requirements, and you can see how this can waste time and create infighting on the team. Even worse, managers who are forced to make purely subjective decisions can be seen as weak leaders or playing to favorites. After the decision is made, someone wins, and the other party loses out. Without an objective basis point for a decision, the leaders are really participating in eroding trust even while trying their best to solve the problem. If everyone uses the CRM tool and follows basic standards on how to document activity, rules of client and candidate ownership can be established. These guidelines then become standard operating procedure followed by all, which builds trust. WeCulture is about promoting teamwork and employee engagement. In addition to promoting trust, standard documentation allowed us to leverage several operational efficiencies, saving us time and money. Recruiters could review opened job orders in our CRM tool, and standard documentation allowed them to effectively represent opportunities to candidates. Because all our clients and candidates were now in the database, we could manage marketing campaigns for maximum impact. We can create strategies for how we engage customers as a team and have objective measures of progress. The KPI's we took time to make the foundation of Pedal the Bike are tracked and accurately reflect team effort.

7. *"Better teams make better players. They have people who care about the success of the business and work together."*
WeCulture is part of the business for a specific purpose: to drive results through teamwork. As we hire the right people based on core values and core qualities, they will need training along the way. This tenet is a reminder that every colleague is part of creating our culture with the responsibility to help others perform at their best. While this reinforces a thought process centered around a coaching environment, it also speaks to peer accountability. As colleagues execute, their actions can have an impact on the rest of the team. In the chapter on Pedal the Bike, we tracked individual KPI's but also have this roll up into a larger team goal. We talk about Millennials wanting to be part of the bigger picture, a task that contributes to overall success. If the team is focused on pushing each other at a peer level to achieve the goal, this encourages individuals to reach outside their comfort zones to do their parts.

We already established that recruiters and sales professionals have a codependent relationship. Why do we need to remind the colleagues that "better teams make better players"? This is so experienced salespeople will take time to work with a rookie recruiter going over what a qualified candidate resume looks like, some good questions to ask to screen for the role, or discuss the selling points about their client. Experienced recruiters will take time to coach a rookie salesperson through taking an effective job order or review the details on the selling points of a great candidate for the client presentation. This reminder is necessary. Let's say this type of peer coaching and accountability did not happen. I'm sure managers would catch some of these learning opportunities in real time but certainly not all of them. Salespeople don't have to coach new recruiters, but if new recruiters are better at finding the right candidates, we have more product to fill job orders. Recruiters don't have to coach a rookie salesperson how to present a good candidate, but if they do, that candidate has a better chance of being interviewed and is closer to a placement.

This tenet is a reminder that if we all work together, we make each other better. It supports WeCulture's core value of Be Positive and promotes teamwork through effective execution to drive results.

8. **"Live the company core values."**

    We took the time to look up our parent company's core values and agreed that they should be included in WeCulture. As WeCulture becomes part of any organization, we must keep the things in our identity that make the company what it is today. This tenet was added as we began rolling out WeCulture beyond my region. Even though my offices had core values via WeCulture, our division did not have published core values, so we borrowed from our parent company to make this connection. Our team believed that the company core values were well-aligned and fit well with what we accomplished leveraging WeCulture. "Cool head" means we stay calm under pressure; "warm heart" is a reminder to treat others with compassion; "working hands" shows that we all contribute through effort.

9. **"Our goal is to have every colleague make more money than last year."**

    This one is my favorite. In a sales environment, the primary motivator is increasing personal income, and we includes me too. ☺ It is the job of every leader in a commission sale to make every effort to help their colleagues achieve financial success, and we took this tenet very seriously. This tenet is a critical reminder to drive results and that this focus is mutually beneficial for colleagues, the team, and the organization.

As discussed in chapter two, when I took the job, our colleagues were not meeting performance standards, which also means their personal incomes were below their own expectations. As we put focus on working together and execution of standard operating procedures and KPI's, it was critical we spoke to how this effort helped them. As sales started to turn around, we created tools to project personal income, illustrating how the real-time results would impact future earnings. Weekly one-on-one meetings had new meaning for the team. We would plug in last week's sales to an income-tracking spreadsheet and show how one consulting placement would impact annual earnings, and it became a great motivation tool. During annual planning sessions, we could map out how KPI activity can drive earnings, showing how many placements were needed to hit the individuals desired income target. We could set goals for gross profit, average bill rates, and number of direct-hire placements and then use the projections to manage real time each week. If we make two extra consulting placements in December that carry into next year, how does it impact income for the individuals? Now we know; now it has meaning.

I managed that office for three years and am proud to say that every year each colleague made more money than the prior year. Over the three years, several more than doubled their personal annual income. This tenet really helped us tie it all together, boiling WeCulture down to real results and change for each colleague. Pedal the Bike has new meaning. As we stated, WeCulture is not about some touchy-feely nonsense. WeCulture is about driving financial results for the company and impacting colleagues' personal incomes in a positive way. All this focus on increasing personal incomes had great residual impact. This office grew and exceeded budget all three years. Because of this, each year I made more money than last year...we included me too.

10. *"Professional Development is part of every 1 on 1."*
The best organizations focus on training and professional development. As Baby Boomers retire at a rate of ten-thousand-plus a day and the next generation of workers joins the team, training will be critical. In the book *Flawless Execution* by James D. Murphy, a key takeaway is how training can impact the business. Murphy is an F-15 fighter pilot who now runs a successful business-

consulting practice, and in the book, he is surprised that CEOs feel training is something time-consuming or unnecessary. In the world of fighter pilots, training saves lives. Seconds matter, and having actions become second nature through simulated activity makes each pilot one with their machine. My takeaway from reading that was how effectively the team executes matters just as much as the actual act of execution. Even in the most routine tasks, activity effectiveness matters just as much as the activity itself. If we invoice one hundred clients, getting paid timely depends on the invoices being prepared correctly. If we invoice the wrong amount, have the wrong payment terms, or invoice weekly when our contract states that invoices are done monthly, we will be paid late or not at all. How we execute a task matters as much as the act of doing it.

We discussed strategies on executing training for WeCulture in the last chapter. This tenet is a reminder for our team that professional development is a never-ending commitment to our success. Part of our hiring process is selling our company to prospective candidates, and through the process, the team will review WeCulture. Task-level training is only part of what this actually means. The best teams make the best players, and professional development is designed to help individuals grow soft skills. I worked with a top producer, and this person was a great sales professional. His clients loved him, and these relationships created great opportunities with our business. Unfortunately this salesperson was all about "I" and not "we." As much as the recruiters appreciated all the opportunities to fill job orders, they would roll their eyes as this salesperson talked — quotes like "I filled this job order," not "we filled this job order." When a candidate did not win the job on the interview, he would say to recruiters, "You could have prepped your candidate better." After observing this behavior and getting feedback from other colleagues, we spent time in each one-on-one talking through different ways to approach situations. We worked on use of language, proper use of pronouns, and how to deliver feedback performance to recruiters. "We" fill jobs, recruiters find candidates for the jobs sales people bring in. Candidate prep is done by both colleagues; "we" could have done a better job preparing our candidate. We also did coaching sessions together to teach this sales professional how to lead a meeting for solving a problem (tenet #5). Professional development is our means of reinforcing how we practice WeCulture to drive results.

11. *"Hire diverse teams focused on core qualities: intelligence, communication skills, thought process, and DRIVE."*

We devoted an entire chapter to hiring based on WeCulture core values and core qualities. This tenet addresses diversity in the workplace and is listed as a reminder to hire the most-qualified people for the company. Our internal staff should be a direct reflection of the diversity in our market and focused on core values and core-quality match. Some organizations evaluate applicants based on criteria that should not impact performance. Being in staffing for almost twenty years, I have met human-resources professionals who are the biggest offenders, rejecting people based on age, nationality, visa status, and a variety of other reasons that have nothing to do with core values or core qualities. Aside from this being unethical and illegal, these discriminatory practices can have a negative impact on performance. People from diverse backgrounds have different ideas and will appeal to different external audiences. If we "typecast" our team, we limit our thinking and client/candidate base. Narrow thinking and a narrow client base equal less opportunity. "We" includes everyone who fits our core values and core qualities, and because this is one of our tenets, the business I was charged to lead had people from all walks of life. This supports our core value Honest and Ethical to drive results.

WeCulture is about leveraging core values to drive results through employee engagement. As we grew, these tenets are how we personalized WeCulture to the needs of our business and made it consistent from office to office. The posters were only the beginning of our public display of WeCulture. Soon we had WeCulture gear. Our first item was a lapel pin. I ordered 250 of these and started by wearing one every day. As I traveled office to office and attended meetings at headquarters, people would ask what it was and could they have one. I used the opportunity to introduce WeCulture and shared that we give out the lapel pin when people display a WeCulture core value through personal action. As I saw WeCulture catch on, I would send out lapel pins with personal notes to colleagues all over the country and coined the phrase "We Includes You." If I could see the individual in person, we would present WeCulture giveaway items at morning job-order meetings and say a few words about why we recognized the colleague. Soon we had a signature picker (see below), then we did apparel, (golf shirt, wristbands, fleece vest), and WeCulture took hold. Our WeCulture gear created awareness and supported our core value of Be Positive by catching people doing the right thing in the moment. When we did the signature picker, it started with me and my SVP putting it in our electronic signatures on internal email. Within two weeks, we saw it on signatures for almost 50 percent of our teams, and people wanted more. Tenets drive our vision, supported by positive reinforcement of desired behaviors.

As we move on through the next chapters, we will focus on how leaders can nurture WeCulture through their own actions. As we learned in chapter two, we all create the culture, but the leader must be the guide.

"Practice is the hardest part of learning, and training is the essence of transformation."

— Ann Voskamp

CHAPTER NINE
TRAINING TO DRIVE GROWTH

So far we have reviewed core values to drive action, how to leverage WeCulture for hiring, the importance of standard operating procedures, and how to incorporate tenets to guide your own vision. WeCulture is taking shape, and we have a basic blueprint to share with our colleagues. As we move forward, how we execute will impact results, and based on this, we need to support our core values and tenets with training. Activity levels are a key performance indicator, and training determines how effectively each activity is performed by the team. High-volume activity without quality is not the goal; we want meaningful actions to drive financial results.

In the book *Grit* by Angela Duckworth, talent is the myth promoted by leaders that ability is something people have or do not have. It often becomes the excuse for failure as we justify the inability to compete with talent being the reason for success. The truth of the matter is talent is stagnant without effort. If we work with our colleagues and apply effort through training to raw, desired, core qualities, we can develop the skills to succeed. Training is a form of team effort where the organization partners with the individual to develop the necessary skills to succeed. The myth of talent can be dispelled, creating a level playing field for any willing participant.

Working for large, publicly traded companies, most executives look at activity in simple terms: more activity = more results. The reality is that this is only true when the current activity levels are yielding desired results. When it comes to execution, quality of actions and techniques matter. In a manufacturing plant, volume can be at the highest levels, yet if we have higher than expected material waste or low quality requiring rework to meet standards, then driving higher activity levels might hurt the organization. Pushing higher activity levels yields more rework and more waste. If we train staff on following procedure and techniques to reduce waste and improve quality, we can lower costs while maintaining the same level of activity. Cost savings through reduced waste and rework have a direct, positive impact to profits. Other benefits can include reduced overtime costs through efficiency, as well as less rework, meaning a greater percentage of product produced meets quality standards — more product for the same effort and more satisfied customers.

In sales how we execute our daily activities has a direct impact on close rates, the percentage of prospects that actually become a sale. With more complex products or services, we can impact the length of a sales cycle to close. Think about the boost to morale if the same level of KPI's yields more sales faster. If we really examine what drives financial results, activity levels are only part of the equation. Often an increase in activity levels will offer a small, short-lived improvement in results. Sustainable results are driven through a constant effort to improve activity at the task level with a focus on efficiency and quality.

Most organizations talk a great game when it comes to training. They have documented operating procedures, training manuals, online curriculums, classes, and mentor programs. Collectively U.S firms spent over $150 billion in 2015 according to the 2015 Training Industry Report. Yet with all the money spent for some organizations, training has little impact on results. Is it the material? Our delivery? The trainers? Maybe, but good leaders will hold themselves accountable first. The leaders are ultimately responsible for the success or failure of the team. With all the money spent, along with time and effort, how can we train more effectively? Let's look at the situation below.

The staffing business is a great example to illustrate how quality of execution is just as important as overall volume of activity. I learned this first hand as an RVP leading two locations that had direct hire services. Direct hire is when a client hires a candidate referred by our company and pays a percentage of the starting salary as a fee. We had a team of seven executive recruiters between the two locations and were billing an average of $70,000 in fees each month. Our expected per-desk average billing was $20,000 per month — or a team goal of $140,000. Like most managers, I asked for more calls and job orders...let's create more opportunities to drive sales. Makes sense, right? As we focused our effort to increase KPI's, we pulled more job orders but failed to improve our revenue results. New hires came and went, and the cost of turnover was hurting our profits and morale. As I started to dig deeper into day-to-day operations of this division, it became clear that our order volume was actually above the standard for each colleague. Our outbound-call volume was also ranked in the top three each week. The problem was not how many job orders we had or the volume of outbound activity; the issue was that this team had the lowest close ratios in the company. If we have the volume of jobs needed to grow, working with this team on technique could change everything.

We started weekly trainings on specific topics, role-playing to hone our skills. This was coupled with call blocks as a team to execute new techniques in real time. How we take a job order from a client matters more than how many job orders we get. We focused on understanding the why behind a hiring need and the client's specific hiring process. The hiring process refers to the steps needed from introductions, interviews, offer, client onboarding, and a clearly defined start date. We reviewed how to sell an opportunity to a candidate, how to understand a candidate's specific needs, and methods to coach both parties through each step. Even when delivering a formal offer, how we communicate is just as critical as what we communicate. If both clients and candidates had a complete picture of the hiring process, both parties could logically work through predictable steps to a defined start date. We also revisited all opened requirements that were not moving forward to requalify the requirement using our new approach. Immediately our team started to close more job orders, increasing our fees — success!

Unfortunately it was short-lived. Two months later our close rates dropped, and soon we were right back where we started. As I looked to why, I eliminated the colleagues as a possible cause. KPI's were still exceeding standards, and for a short period of time, we saw the desired financial results. Obviously the team was capable of improving close rates and executing on the training we provided. The missing component was management involvement. The spike came while I was personally involved and training the team each week with the division directors. The increased communication fostered spot coaching and discussion to keep everyone focused on what was learned. Once we saw the desired results, we moved on to the next business challenge without leaving a process behind for accountability and continued learning. Without a system to reinforce the new techniques learned, our team quickly fell back into old habits, taking our results with them.

Realizing this critical error, we went back into training mode, but this time we worked with the team to set up a system to support what was learned, making it part of our culture. We set up a system of two meetings done weekly: a team job-order review and weekly, region-wide call to discuss pending offers from clients to candidates. Pending is defined as an offer we expect to get from our client for a candidate within the next five business days. With these consistent meetings, we created a peer forum for the team to discuss opened requirements and pending offers. Colleagues could work together and hold each other accountable to what they were learning. More important was that as long as the meetings were held, the training was reinforced to become consistent work habits. On average it takes a person between sixty to seventy days to make a behavior become habit. Putting a process in place promoted team learning to drive sustained results. A residual impact was that we now had a scalable process for new hires, a mechanism for our training to be part of the culture owned by our tenured colleagues. This time as our close rates improved, so did our monthly billings. Soon after we had the number-two producing office, and several members of our team were on track for Circle of Excellence awards. Two of our winners were rookies. What is the takeaway?

Training alone is not enough. In the example above, our team was capable of learning, and the missing component was continued engagement from the leader. Without a system to promote execution, learning would be lost. The cadence of meetings promoted discussion and active involvement for the team. As we helped each other close deals, we were building trust through consistently executing techniques to close deals in real time. It took more than the right curriculum to get results. Training is not about teaching; it is about creating work habits. In order for training to create the desired work habits, it must be a total team effort. We includes all colleagues, going beyond trainers and trainees. WeCulture is about driving results through employee engagement.

In the book *Flawless Execution* by James D. Murphy, training is the critical component for promoting standards of excellence, consistency, and continued improvement. One key takeaway from the book was that practice through routine training makes perfect. In briefing meetings, fighter pilots will role-play through execution of a mission. Simulated missions are done consistently, regardless of levels of experience, to keep skills razor sharp. For a fighter pilot, a lapse in judgement or failure to execute in even the most routine mission can mean life or death. In their world, flawless execution is not nice to have, and it is not just a stated goal — it saves lives. In business the same principles can be applied to drive results. Training on desired skills regularly makes things second nature. Once things are second nature, training is necessary to avoid experienced staff taking shortcuts. One example in the book talked about experienced fighter pilots ignoring fuel warnings on missions. After all, the warning comes on, and there is a small time buffer built in to ensure pilots have enough fuel to return from the mission. Maybe we start ignoring the warning and pushing a bit further each time. Before you know it, a plane is lost (and maybe the pilot) all because we know what to do but failed to immediately execute. In the example above for our direct-hire team, without continued training to reinforce results, old habits and shortcuts took hold, and we lost revenue as a result.

When working for large companies, I would be in meetings to review results, and often training became a common prescription to spot-treat a business deficiency. We would leave the room and go back, teaching our teams a technique to solve a tactical problem and then move on. When the desired results did not magically materialize, senior leaders would be frustrated, often doubting the trainers, the curriculum, or the colleagues and field leaders charged to execute. The truth is, how we deliver training, along with how we reinforce behaviors, is the issue. Let's take a different approach and make training an ongoing, sustained effort. Below is a great example of how a company recognized their own shortcomings in the training process and took action to change it. I was a participant in executing both models and felt the experience could help us understand how training can impact employee engagement.

After three years with the company we discussed in chapter two, they realized that their training was completely ineffective and inconsistent. Each field office was responsible to train new colleagues in their own way, and each quarter we would host a three-day, off-site, new-hire training. Our corporate training team would take colleagues from around the country to review basic tactics of execution and then send the employees back to the field offices. Members of the field leadership team would participate as facilitators in a rotation, and several times during my tenure I would make the trip to HQ to do my part. Sounds like a good plan, and the company made this training trip a big selling point for new hires. As hard as we worked to train new hires during this meeting, field execution was horribly inconsistent from market to market, and turnover was at an all-time high for the enterprise. This process was ineffective for several reasons.

First, colleagues were required to attend regardless of past experience or tenure with our company. We would have a mixed group at various stages of development. The prerequisite to attend was to complete hours of online, self-directed learning that was completely outdated. We knew little about attendees, and they knew very little about us. Three days passed quickly, and facilitators would send home subjective scorecards to field managers, grading colleagues. Aside from three days not being near enough time to evaluate a colleague, these evaluations were often challenged by field leaders as inaccurate. Some leaders would avoid sending their hires just to avoid the grading system they believed to be nonsense.

Second was the curriculum itself. The training focused almost exclusively on tactical-level task execution. We were teaching each colleague from a PowerPoint deck in a class setting, layering in a role-play as needed. We would review the company history while colleagues yawned through the first morning. Then we spent 2½ days lecturing 90 percent of the time. Third, at no point during the training did we incorporate the company core values. Now I understood why when I arrived at this company no one could share what the corporate core values were. We did not even review them during new-hire training. It is impossible to drive desired behavior by leveraging core values if we don't share what they are with our colleagues. Lastly, strategic goals were usually left out. Sometimes we reviewed them — other times, not so much. If Millennials are motivated by being part of the bigger picture and greater good, we were missing the mark.

The training was expensive and largely ineffective. The trip cost four thousand to six thousand dollars per hire, billed back to the field office. Colleagues returned to market and had mixed feedback on the experience, which was largely dependent on the field leader facilitating. Many employees struggled to articulate key takeaways, and field managers had no mechanism in place to reinforce what was learned. Other than a trip to HQ and maybe making new friends, it was back to business as usual. The goal of effective execution to drive results was unrealized despite time, money, and effort.

The good news was the company recognized this challenge and decided to do something about it. Our training leader formed a committee, and this team created a training curriculum for the first one hundred days of employment for all field staff. This training was by far the most comprehensive product I had ever seen in the corporate world and helped us educate employees through active engagement. Below we can look at the reasons why.

CORE VALUES AND LONG-TERM STRATEGY IN MIND

Spot-coaching is critical to help teams stay on track and with true intentions can build relationships among colleagues. For sustained results, training should be part of the overall strategy to ensure time and energy spent contributes to short- and long-term company goals. Learning should not be the only goal of training. This effort should be designed to inspire and motivate trainees, incorporating core values, which are the foundation of what drives behavior in WeCulture. If we hire for core values and core qualities first, then chances are our new hires will have a lot to learn about our business — training on operating procedures, techniques, how to leverage internal resources, use of systems, and, of course, professional development. The 100-Day training course tied in strategy, outlining long-term company goals and how each colleague's role contributed to our overall success. The value of Pedal the Bike was layered in with a gradual ramp into KPI activity levels. There was a points system and financial incentives to exceed goals. As learning decreased, activity levels increased until target KPI goals were reached. Trainees could execute techniques learned in real time to drive sales.

MEANINGFUL CONTENT

Because the training was company-wide and started on day one, we now had consistent training for each new colleague. Under our legacy training, strategy curriculum was largely left to field managers (direct supervisors) to teach new hires the basics of our business before they were sent to the HQ training. One hundred field leaders would work one-on-one with their own direct reports with a few basic tools to guide them. This created challenges. First, some field leaders are more skilled than others, have more time than others, and, frankly, value training more than others. If we asked ten managing directors what the first ten days looked like for a new colleague, we would get ten different answers. How we prepare new hires ties in directly to the services we provide to clients and candidates. With the new plan in place and a well-scripted curriculum, every colleague learned agreed-upon operating procedures along with best practices to succeed. Every aspect of the business was covered, helping new hires execute consistently. Now as we increased activity, new hires would achieve financial results faster — not just more calls but more effective calls and more effective client meetings, all leading to placements. It is the company's responsibility to provide great training, and the new hire is responsible to learn and execute.

ACTIVE ENGAGEMENT THROUGH A TEAM APPROACH

The training committee set a system in place where every field leader would participate to contribute to the learning of every new hire. This was a two-prong approach designed to actively engage colleagues and field leaders for the long haul. First, field managers (managing directors) were ultimately responsible for all learning and activity over the hundred days. This changed their role from content creation to accountability for learning and execution. Much of the learning required role-playing and on-the-job activities that new hires were required to complete with their manager. All activities were set in a daily curriculum, providing a consistent road map to follow. Aside from providing structure for learning, this created a forum for leaders to regularly engage new hires. The bond built can improve employee retention, reducing costly turnover.

Second was that each field leader in the company had to own a specific training topic as part of a team. These topics included learning technology, tactical best practices, standard operating procedures, and overall strategy. Each module was prepared and content executed via a set schedule built into each new 100-Day class via a live, online video session. Nothing was ever prerecorded, and each facilitation team actively delivered content to new hires across the organization. This was a great way to promote employee engagement for leaders and new colleagues. New hires got to interact with leaders over several meetings outside of their own direct supervisor, helping build a deeper bond to the company. Leaders were now not only taking an active role in developing their own hires, but field leaders were actively engaging new hires across the enterprise. For me personally,

I gained a new sense of ownership to the training process. Through the process, I developed relationships with new hires in other markets and naturally took an interest in their success. Some would contact me for questions or extra time on my topic, and it helped us build relationships that would never exist otherwise. Now an entire village of field leaders would be investing in new hires. Not only were we actively engaging new hires, but we were also engaging our field leaders — consistent, active reinforcement of core processes and best practices to promote flawless execution.

WeCulture is focused on employee engagement, embracing core values to grow the business. Training offers the perfect opportunity to engage teams at all levels within the organization. The example above was a great success and helped the organization retain well-trained colleagues. To maximize the impact of learning offered through training, it will require a strategic approach. Why we train staff and how we deliver training will determine how effective what we teach is actually retained. Goals for training should have a focus beyond learning: building each colleague's relationship to the organization and leaders.

In the example above, we can incorporate the core values of Pedal the Bike through executing activity in real time as we learn. This core value is not just about higher volume of activity — it is about connecting activity to the desired end result. Nothing reinforces a technique taught better than having someone execute in a real-world situation. Knowledge is built through learning; confidence grows through successful execution. We need to incorporate how people actually retain knowledge, making training go from the classroom to the real world. Let's look at adult-learning retention based on methods used to deliver content.

Adult-learning retention stats

- Lecture = 5 percent
- Reading = 10 percent
- Demonstration = 30 percent
- Group = 50 percent
- Practical Execution (Experiential) = 75 percent
- Teaching Others = 90 percent

How people learn and retain information can be directly tied to how we execute training. To actively engage trainees and trainer, it is critical that there is active involvement. Online, prerecorded training has become very popular. It is easy for companies to execute an online curriculum and inexpensive to deliver. Unfortunately ease of use and low cost will leave new colleagues retaining only about 5 to 10 percent of content, which will impact on-the-job performance. In addition to low retention rates, managers can often outsource training new colleagues to this online portal. More time spent learning online alone means less time bonding with your new leader and teammates.

For the new 100-Day Training, we focused on live demonstrations, group activities, and experiential training tactics for new hires, taking average content-retention rates to about 60 percent. With high levels of retained learning and managers retaining 90 percent of content through teaching others, it was easy to see why hires under the new training would ramp to financial goals faster. Our retention rates also improved through active employee engagement built into the process.

In our environment, a tenet of WeCulture was focused on professional development to keep training as a critical part of driving results. To promote a healthy approach to training for your organization, you can structure programs with the below in mind:

- All people can learn and grow professionally, regardless of age or experience. It is the job of the leader to create this vision for training.
- Present all skills as something that can be learned and executed by all.
- Don't allow those with talent to be excused from training. Without learning, your best people will not get better; in some cases, an overinflated self-image can hurt overall execution of process.
- Provide feedback in a positive way to promote learning and build a bond among colleagues.
- Leverage all staff to train on their specific area of expertise and practice execution with new colleagues to reinforce what was learned.
- As a leader, open your mind to your own need and ability to learn for professional growth. Let your actions as a trainer sharpen your own skills.

Training is a never-ending process for all colleagues at all levels in the organization. WeCulture's mission is focused on employee engagement embracing core values to grow the business. Trainings should incorporate measurable activity as colleagues learn (Pedal the Bike), motivate colleagues through regular interaction (Be Positive), and encourage everyone to be Honest and Ethical. For leaders "we" includes you, and the success of any training depends on your own execution, positive energy, and focus on ethics. You can set the tone through your own behavior with WeCulture in mind to set the example that can be followed by others.

"You will never see eye-to-eye if you never meet face-to-face."
— Warren Buffett

CHAPTER TEN

WECULTURE FOR EFFECTIVE MEETINGS

Meetings are the part of everyday life in business that can shape and define culture for organizations regardless of industry. If we all kept a log of weekly activity, we would come to realize that we spend a great deal of time working interacting with our colleagues in scheduled meetings. As an RVP, my own calendar had at least twelve hours per week devoted exclusively to recurring meetings, conference calls, WebEx, and one-on-ones. Studies show that the average professional in the U.S. spends about 35 percent of his or her time in group meetings. Many of you reading this are probably counting out all the hours spent over the past few days devoted to meetings. As you are thinking about it, how many of these meetings were productive? Which were effective? Ineffective? How many meetings have you attended in your career wishing you could have the time back to spend on something else? Over 33 percent of employees consider the meetings they attend to be unproductive. Almost 50 percent of all meetings attended by colleagues are recurring staff meetings. If a third of your team is attending recurring meetings that they feel are unproductive, what impact does this have on morale?

What are some of the most common complaints about meetings?

1. Inconclusive: No decisions made after ideas are vetted and discussed by the team.

2. Poor Preparation: Leaders don't have an agenda or share it with colleagues, leaving no time to prepare.
3. Disorganized: No clear objectives or path to achieve a result.
4. Individuals Dominate: Leaders take center stage, or colleagues use it as a forum to push an ego-driven agenda.
5. Win/Lose Approach: Best ideas are lost to colleagues determined to win above the greater good.
6. No Published Results or Follow-Up: Meetings end without next steps or assigned to-do's.
7. Too Long: Discussions go on without end, and because of this, meetings rarely end on time.
8. Meetings don't start on time.

WeCulture is about leveraging core values to drive behavior. With meetings being a large part of how colleagues spend their time at work, along with a critical part of how an organization will drive results, how well we execute will impact employee engagement.

MEETINGS AND WECULTURE CORE VALUES

Leaders can start by measuring meetings against the three core values. Core values are used to drive behavior and can help us set the stage for team interactions. With so much time spent in scheduled meetings, conference calls, or WebEx, they can set the tone for how well the organization will execute. Impact can be felt both internally and externally to the company. As we drive results, innovation, or better products and services through successful meetings, we will attract and retain more customers. If we change the way our teams look at meetings, they can become an active tool for positive employee engagement.

Great meetings should move us closer to achieving our goals, and WeCulture's core value of Pedal the Bike can be used to guide. Ask yourself as you schedule your next meeting: How will this gathering help us move closer to achieving a long- or short-term goal? Pedal the Bike is about executing activities as a team to move forward. If we are going to gather a group and take them away from daily activity, the time needs to be as productive as possible. Be Positive should always be considered as a critical part of the process. While meetings should have quantifiable goals, they should also be motivating, including a call to action for those participating. Having colleagues leave knowing their roles going forward, along with action items, will keep the focus on the greater good. Applying Core Value #3 can make or break team meetings. The success of the organization depends on those making crucial decisions having access to accurate information. Meetings need to be about the exchange of ideas. More often than not, this is where meetings fail and can ultimately derail initiatives critical to success. In the book *Five Dysfunctions of a Team* by Patrick Lencioni, the author describes a fictional team that is failing through the cadence of meetings under the leadership of a new CEO. One observation was that the groups would not share ideas, and the reasons all led back to issues with trust or ego. As the new CEO addressed the issues of trust and ego, meetings became more effective, and their failing organization found its way back to a path of growth.

How can we incorporate core values to create effective meetings? We can leverage process designed to address the specific reasons colleagues find meeting unproductive and demotivating.

HAVE A MISSION STATEMENT

A mission statement is the specific reason we are calling the meeting in the first place. Meetings could be called to solve a problem, to review milestones on projects, conduct training, or review results. Being in sales for over twenty years, I have adopted this approach to internal meetings because it works so well for external client meetings. I would never visit a client without an objective or end goal in mind, and I would open each client meeting with a purpose statement. Simply put, if we are having a meeting, we should tell the participants why. Keeping our core values in mind, this lets participants know what we are trying to accomplish. If they are going to put in effort (Pedal the Bike), it would help to know the destination or end goal. It also speaks to Core Value #3 Honest and Ethical. If we are transparent regarding why we are meeting, it can take away stress, allowing colleagues to come prepared.

Case in point: I worked for a company for over eight years, and when I became an RVP, my new boss was the queen of meetings. I would often get the call on a Friday to book a flight to her home office to meet. I would ask her what was up, and she would reply, "Nothing important. Just book the flight and hotel and send me your itinerary." I would spend the entire weekend trying to figure out what we would cover for these meetings, and it would create a ton of stress. From my point of view, this was done to keep her subordinates off balance. I would show up usually to a printed binder of data that she reviewed and I would be seeing for the first time. I'm a pretty confident guy and can perform very well under pressure, but it took me awhile to get used to this style of leadership to perform at my best. Not knowing the purpose of the meeting also created issues with trust. I would spend the first hour or so of the meeting trying to figure out why I was there, what data we were reviewing, and what we hoped to accomplish. I know what you are thinking: *Hey Chris, why not just ask her?* I did every time. I hear senior leaders say things like, "We need to be a little unpredictable to keep people on their toes." Her favorite was that the leaders reporting to me should have a small amount of fear as motivation. The tactic worked — I was off balance coming into meetings more often than not. The residual impact was that as time passed, my trust in her diminished.

I took a big lesson away to apply to WeCulture. Anytime I invite a colleague to meet, I share the reason why without exception. It can be one-on-one meetings or large group meetings — the reason why always promotes productivity, allowing colleagues to come prepared. It also helps us weed out team members not pedaling the bike. If you know the reason for the meeting and do not take time to prepare, then that is on you. Usually this will happen once with a new colleague because most organizations have ineffective meetings. Once a new hire sees the team in action, they catch on quickly and do their part. When it comes to meeting prep, "we includes you."

CHOOSING PARTICIPANTS

Once we have a defined mission or purpose for the meeting, we can make a list of who should attend based on what needs to be accomplished. Publicly traded companies use a classic method which, from my point a view, is a main reason nothing ever gets done. Meeting attendees are decided based on titles or rank. The worst part about being an RVP was all the meetings I had to attend because of my title. Hours of my life lost in a place where my opinion did not matter or I could add little to no value. Often these meetings would generate more meetings because we would not have the key people on hand to provide critical information. At times leaders attending would participate in discussions where they had no expertise. Executives would suppress open and honest discussion with their presence. I heard this statement countless times or some version of it: "I would have brought that up but did not want to put a colleague on the spot with our CEO in the room." Some executives lack patience to see issues worked through by the team and often cannot help themselves to push a process along. If issues are not discussed with all information available or honest debate, there can be unproductive outcomes. First, the team will not take action if issues are not vetted; without discussion nothing happens. Second (and even worse) is that the team decides on action based on incomplete information, making the effort take us off course from our mission — resources, time, and money spent on work that has a negative impact.

To avoid these pitfalls, invite colleagues based on a few basic criteria. First, include resources who have the expertise we need to move the mission forward. This could be anyone, regardless of title or role. An example: If we are talking about customer-experience survey results in a car dealership, I would immediately include the person greeting customers at the front desk. Why? This person is part of the customer experience and will usually have a view of the showroom floor, quietly observing a big part of the customer experience. Second, include key stakeholders or representation if the group is too large. This could be internal customers, business-side users, or client-facing staff impacted by the mission. Lastly, I would include the final decision maker. If a project requires approvals for spending or work to progress, best we include the person who has to sign off. Maybe the decision maker will not be invited to every meeting, but the more they see along the way will make getting needed approval easier. Key decision makers often get invited to a final meeting with participants looking for a go/no go on an initiative. Because the decision maker did not see the effort put in along the way or see the evolution of what was done, getting buy-in will become more of a sales pitch. Some executives driven by ego will ask for changes just to make their mark, slowing down or taking the project off track. If decision makers see projects unfold along the way, this active engagement will increase their commitment and buy-in. This makes the approval process based on facts and overall return on investment rather than a sales pitch. As an RVP, I would often be a designated decision maker and always appreciated being included on the evolution of a project.

SET AN AGENDA

If we know the reason why we are meeting, then we should set the tone with the agenda. A good agenda will keep the discussion on track and guide the team toward the mission objective we set in step one. A great tip for leaders is to seek input from a few participants to help you create the agenda. Second, distribute the agenda prior to the meeting. In sales we have weekly one-on-ones with all colleagues, which are done by appointment for about an hour. I distribute invites with the agenda attached. Good agendas will have a clear path to promote discussion, assigned colleagues to lead topics, and a timeframe devoted to each item listed. Agendas also allow colleagues to dig deeper into the mission statement and focus preparation. A well-prepared team can stay on point, and with lots of information on hand, discussion (and decisions) can be based on facts rather than politics or ego. Assigning agenda items to participants will help create buy-in from your colleagues, and the residual benefit is that it will help foster one of our tenets on professional development.

For recurring meetings, I recommend the agenda include specific fixed items to review and time for structured, open discussion. If there are action items from the last meeting, these should be reviewed as the first topic. Think about project milestone meetings; these could be weekly or monthly and should include specific next steps to move the project forward. Any data we are using to measure progress should be shared in a consistent format. The data should support progress outlined as reported in the review of action items. Issues, challenges, and general discussion should be next. A tip is to list out any known discussion topics in the agenda prior to the meeting. As issues are discussed, this should bring action items to assign for the next meeting. Project teams often use dashboards, and there are several technology tools to choose from. Color coding a dashboard to measure progress from meeting to meeting not only helps track progress but can also be used as a motivation tool.

ACTION ITEMS

Pedal the Bike is a core value of WeCulture, and how we manage to-do or action items for meetings is critical to how we achieve results. Nothing will happen unless we define the tasks that need to be completed. Colleagues see meetings as ineffective because decisions are not made and often we have no clear path forward. Issues are discussed, solutions may be agreed on, but meetings end with no defined action. Colleagues walk away from the meeting confused or demotivated, recognizing that the issues have no clear steps to move forward. For me personally, this was the top reason I found meetings to be ineffective. With all the talk about what is not working or what needs to be done, someone must be assigned to take action.

WeCulture was a guide for our offices, and our team used to joke about action items in our meetings — "time to put some real work in." Our strategy was simple. Any issue discussed had to end with specific action items, each assigned to one person for ownership. One owner is critical even if it requires the effort of multiple colleagues. With one owner, now a specific individual is ultimately responsible and can be held accountable. This person can also develop his or her own skills leading other resources to get the job done. We would make a list, taking notes during meetings, and also set a defined due date. This is how we made each meeting speak to WeCulture Core Value "Be Positive." A call to action addresses many of the reasons why colleagues don't find meetings effective. To-do's can motivate participants by giving them meaningful work to contribute to the greater good. As the action items are completed, we make the results public, recognizing those who contribute. Starting meetings reviewing assigned action items make meetings motivating and worth attending. If colleagues are invited to meetings to report on progress of action items assigned to them, it will increase their overall levels of engagement.

START ON TIME/END ON TIME

Football coach Tom Coughlin is one of my favorites. It is not because I'm a New York Giants fan, and he brought the team two championships; it is because he believed in discipline to drive results. I remember when he took over as head coach for the Giants. The local press in New York would publish quotes from sources inside the team organization on the first step to establish order. Meetings always started exactly on time in Coughlin's world. If you were right on time on this team, you were late. Nothing sets the tone for an organization more than starting on time. Let the clock help you create the expectation that what we are trying to accomplish is important. Starting on time is not an issue of respect to the leader; it is about the colleagues sitting next to you. Having this strict rule is the first step in leveling the field that everyone's time is equally important. If you are leading a meeting and a colleague is late, start without them. If it is a key executive, sometimes this can be hard to do and might require a gut check, but if you show people rank allows grace, it can create a double standard. A main reason meetings do not start on time is because participants will show up late.

If you are the most senior person attending a meeting called by a colleague, the best way to support the message is to show up a few minutes early. It will show those you are charged to lead that you care. It also gives you a great opportunity to lead by example; everyone is required to be on time...we includes me too. I remember a meeting we had where our office manager was reviewing one of our first audits. She was nervous and not very comfortable with public speaking. I showed up about ten minutes early while she was preparing in the conference room and made some small talk to help her relax. She was well-prepared and did a great job. I could tell she appreciated the support; at that time, it was really needed.

NO MEETINGS AFTER THE MEETING

This rule is critical to promoting a positive work culture and one that should be followed without exception. The main reason we have a meeting is to vet issues, challenges, and problems and assign action items to move forward. If this is what we expect to happen in our meetings, then there is no reason for side discussion. Organizational politics thrive when meetings are ineffective, and as we mentioned a few times throughout the book, organizational politics is the worst form of culture cancer. Nothing undermines the credibility of leadership and the meetings in an organization more than the perception that the real decisions are made behind closed doors long after the other participants leave the room.

Case in point: I was a managing director at the time, and we had successfully established WeCulture in our office, growing our business 50 percent year over year, making our team one of the most successful offices in the company. As a result, we were asked to take on service for a key national account that was currently failing under the existing team. We were charged to take over two locations and get the account back on track. When we inherited this client, our company was last in the market of ten active vendors. I was excited about the idea — a distressed account with all upside potential while I had a team of colleagues that was achieving great results. What could go wrong? As we engaged the client, I could see why there was a challenge. The major-accounts VP assigned at the time was one of the most political individuals I had ever met. If he participated in a meeting, I would always get calls after the meeting to gossip about what was said or for lobbying his own agenda. The client reviewed vendor results quarterly, and this VP would attend the meeting at the client site. Because of this, his decisions and input always played to the next client quarterly review. We were failing because our company was always putting in stopgap solutions so we could share with the client a change we were making rather than take a long-term approach to solve deeply rooted issues with regard to service. Our staff was aware of this failing strategy, and it was almost impossible to motivate salespeople and recruiters to give their best efforts. Why invest all the time if the VP on the account would blame failure on us and swap us out in the next review?

After the first ninety days, I decided to commit to the sales team put in place calling on the account and would not allow any changes. Consistent salespeople would help us develop relationships to drive sales. The second step was that I ended the practice this VP had of a meeting after the meeting. If I got a call expressing concerns about a colleague's performance, I would stop the conversation and just conference the other employee in. Unfortunately this did not end the meeting-after-the-meeting practice; this VP just started calling someone else. I found out when we had won a large-scale project for fifteen resources in our market. We had a kickoff call with the client, and our sales and recruiting teams felt confident we would easily meet the budget and timeline for hires. About an hour later, I got an email from the CEO of our division. Apparently this account VP reached out, claiming we were not committed to deliver on the project. This was after six months of 100 percent delivery to every requirement assigned to our team and me personally telling the client on the call that we would exceed expectations. Why would this account VP do something so demotivating and counterproductive? This was pretty demotivating, especially since our recruiting director and sales professional were both copied on the email. It was all about his own ego. He told the CEO he had no faith in our effort, and if we failed, it was all on us. If we won, he would step in the spotlight — perfect politics to preserve his own image to the client. This was why our company was failing for so many years with the client. Every decision we made was done after the meeting — behind the curtain — all to protect the one ego-driven VP. By the way, we filled all the roles ahead of the client timeline and on budget. Our team governed its behavior on WeCulture's core values, putting the greater good for our clients and candidate first. It also helped that after that email, our team left this guy off the meeting invites. If a meeting attendee is culture cancer, take away his or her ability to participate — stop inviting them. It was easy to repair the damage done to team morale without this VP around by keeping our team focused on results.

If colleagues won't bring up issues in the meetings, gather feedback as to why. If the reasons are related to pride or ego, address it and make sure that the meeting format creates a tone for honest feedback to be shared. If the colleague still won't share feedback in the meeting while the rest of the team does, it might be best to take them off the list of attendees. This is not always punitive. Sometimes a person just may not be good in a large group, or we could have invited someone not realizing he or she really does not fit the criteria to be a participant. When someone is removed from a meeting invite, be sure to share the reason why. After all, Honest and Ethical is WeCulture Core Value #3.

Meetings can make or break corporate culture, and I recommend that you benchmark your business before making any changes. Self-reflection is the first step to identifying and owning any issues. This is a simple exercise. Go through your calendar in the last six months and list every internal company meeting you have attended. As always, I recommend using a whiteboard (the act of writing this out will help you with the process). Invite three to five members of your team and rate each one in the below categories (yes or no):

1. Defined Mission
2. Clear Agenda
3. Right Attendees
4. Clear Action Items Set and Assigned
5. Start on Time/End on Time
6. No Meeting after the Meeting

As you look at the list and evaluations, how many of these meetings are helping you build a great culture through active employee engagement? Which meetings need an overhaul? Which should be scrapped? Once you have a list, take steps to make changes to ensure the meetings in your work environment are a yes for all six criteria. This process should be ongoing and done every six to twelve months to maximize meetings, driving positive employee engagement. If your colleagues spend the average 35 percent of their time in meetings now, over one-third of all their time is designed to drive results through employee engagement — the prime directive of WeCulture.

In any company large or small, changing the meeting cadence will require patience. If you go through your list and find that sweeping change is needed, it might be best to communicate to the team that you are evaluating the meeting schedule and that changes will be made. Be honest — if you are the reason meetings are failing, then admit it; own up to your part of how amending your own approach is required. People generally resist change. Your managers reporting to you who host their own meetings will need time to adjust. Maybe change a few meetings to a new format to see how things go. The most important thing here is to expect that it takes about ninety days to change behavior. Depending on the current state of your work environment, you should set goals and treat this change as a long-term initiative. After you make a plan, stick to it for at least six months and gather feedback from your colleagues along the way to ensure you are on the right path.

"If your actions inspire others to dream more, learn more, do more and become more, you are a leader."

— *John Quincy Adams*

YOUR PART
TO DRIVE WECULTURE

"I alone cannot change the world, but I can cast a stone across the waters to create many ripples."

— Mother Teresa

CHAPTER ELEVEN
WECULTURE STARTS WITH YOU

As we look to make WeCulture part of the success of any organization, it is important to understand that it all starts with you. In chapter two, we discussed how the team in our office was led to the realization that everyone is responsible to create the culture. In the book *True North* by Bill George, the point is made that professional success is achieved through authenticity. Be who you truly are and join an organization where you have common ground in personal style and core values. The only thing an individual can control is his or her own actions. How we interact with others, solve problems, and personal effort are all governed through our own choices. Having common ground through core values will set the stage to guide the actions taken by individuals; the need for stated core values and tenets can shape and guide behavior. WeCulture is a blueprint that requires action to get the fire going — a spark...that spark is you. Regardless of your position, title, or rank in an organization, you decide who you bring to work each day, and your actions will have an immediate impact on those around you. We create the culture, and we includes you. Why is this so important?

According to a Gallup Poll in July 2015, the average full-time employee in the U.S. works forty-seven hours, which equates to six days a week. For most of us, the majority of our waking hours are spent at work, thinking about work, or related to work. Layer in commuting (the average in the U.S. is 25.4 minutes, according to the U.S. Census Bureau), and the total hours dedicated to work is about fifty-one to fifty-two per week. As a result, how our workdays go often has lasting effects on personal lives, health, and families. Studies show that only about one-third of people actually enjoy their jobs — that means two-thirds don't. Think about it — 66 percent of people are generally indifferent or dissatisfied with their jobs. The influence of dissatisfied employees to society and behavioral norms is almost impossible to measure.

For the workplace, the financial effect is very real. With so many employees in the workforce not fully engaged, the impact to productivity can represent real cost to companies. Another Gallup Poll shows that such a high level of disengaged employees collectively cost U.S. organizations between $450 to $550 billion. Why? Dissatisfied or disengaged employees don't give their best effort; man-hours and the spark of innovation are often lost. Some truly disgruntled employees may actively work against the company goals and, in rare cases, put the enterprise at risk. Take the example of Ashley Madison, a website designed to introduce married people to have extramarital affairs. For obvious reasons, protection of client identity and personal information related to using the service is critical to the business model. While you may not approve of Ashley Madison, its web platform had information for about thirty-seven million users, which was hacked and put users at risk. After an investigation, the CEO suggested that the hack could have been the result of a disgruntled employee. The $100-million company may not survive.

For the individual, a general dissatisfaction or indifference to something we spend so much time doing will have impact on the other aspects of our lives. Our personal relationships and health suffer as the stress and anxiety cannot be easily left at the office. Sure, you can spend your free time doing things that make you happy, exercise, eat right...but the fifty-plus hours a week over time will shape who you are outside of work for your friends, family, and your own well-being. If this is not a call to action for change, then nothing else will be.

WeCulture is about creating a great work environment. The mission is focused on employee engagement embracing core values to grow the business. The expectations of employees have changed. Studies show that Millennials rank being part of the greater good and a strong, positive corporate culture a priority over income. We discussed the top reasons employees leave jobs, and bad culture, bad bosses, and negative employees are at the top of the list. I would argue that Baby Boomers and Generation X share this desire to be part of something better as well. So if you want work to be better than it is, time to show it using WeCulture core values to govern your actions. Each one is under your control. Pedal the Bike is about effort, completely governed by the individual. Be Positive — how you look at colleagues, leadership, and challenges is completely under your control. Honest and Ethical — you make the choice to do what is right or wrong each day. These choices have lasting impact. Control what you can control and make sure your actions contribute to making your company a great place to work. The example you set will inspire others and more people to join the cause.

Sometimes our most productive employees can set the worst example. In sales this happens with top performers where ego or leadership's perceived dependence on their productivity allows for exceptions to standard operating procedures or the norm for professional behavior. While their productivity is off the charts, their other behaviors can be a counterbalance that makes them a liability in the long run.

Case in point: Let's look at the career of Latrell Sprewell. Excellent basketball player but better known for his off-court activities. Most notable was his sixty-eight game suspension for choking his coach at practice. Think about this action alone and the impact it could have on the morale of Latrell's team. How could anyone look to him as a trusted partner? Forget any hope of being a role model for rookies entering the league. Think of all the practices or games where he sapped energy, projecting negative energy on those around him. Imagine you are working for a new company and a plant worker walks off the assembly line and begins choking the plant manager. How can the team focus on its work with something like this happening? What is the effect to productivity? Quality?

His career spanned thirteen years. While a great basketball player, he will be remembered more for his volatile behavior and his unceremonious exit from basketball, rejecting a three-year, $21-million extension deal in October 2004. His response to the offer: "I have a family to feed...if Glen Taylor wants to see my family fed, he better cough up some money. Otherwise you're going to see these kids in one of those Sally Struthers commercials soon." He declined the contract and finished his existing contract, playing the worst season of his career. After several other lower offers from teams around the league that were rejected, Latrell never played in the NBA again. In any organization, the greater good of the team must come before ourselves. Clearly Sprewell put himself above the team, allowing his temper to bring a long-term suspension. His inability to work with his employer and to settle in a professional manner on a contract marked the end of his career.

On the other end of the spectrum, your top performers can be champions of team and inspire greatness in those around them. Michael Jordan is one of the best basketball players of all time. The number of championships, MVP awards, and other career highlights are too many to list; he is well-known to all. Michael Jordan is the most decorated player to ever play in the NBA. Even with all his fame, achievements, and endorsements, his legacy is defined by his core values, which inspired those around him. While easily one of the highest-paid athletes of all time, Michael Jordan did not let fame and fortune define him; his focus was always on being a better basketball player. He was a role model for other players, fans, and for those who aspire to play the game of basketball. Because of this, his actions elevated players around him; experts say that during his tenure, the Bulls were one of the greatest teams in NBA history. His core values of hard work, passion, and embracing lessons from failure inspire people to this day. His tireless dedication to being a better player, to never give up, and to be an example of ethical and honest behavior also make him an admired American icon.

If you are a top performer in your company, who do you want to be? Michael Jordan or Latrell Sprewell? If you are a leader, who offers more value long-term to the team? I had a colleague reporting to me for about two years and had to personally ask him that question. I took a promotion to run a larger office in a well-established market. I was with this company for about one year and new to leadership. This office had several top producers through several different lines of business. One division had two top producers who sat next to each other. Their personal production had both of these guys competing each year for the number-one spot out of hundreds of colleagues. Both were truly hardworking and experts at their jobs, setting records year after year. One was quiet and well-liked among the team; working with him was effortless for his peers and for me as his manager. From a leadership standpoint, he was a pleasure to have on the team. The other colleague was a bit different. His production was incredible, and he was with the company several years. He was one of the first employees in the market and often took credit for "managers building a team on my back for years." When we met for the first time, his greeting was, "Nice to meet you. The best way to manage me is to leave me the @&*$ alone." Most of the time he got along with colleagues, but every few weeks, he would have a full-blown tantrum in the middle of our office, which had over fifty colleagues. If he had an issue to address, more often than not, he would erupt in our bullpen, and it would degrade to how underappreciated he was.

As the complaints piled up, my leaders were determined to sweep it under the rug whenever they could. One day I spoke with him, and after acknowledging his truly great productivity and contributions to our company, I asked him, "If we were a basketball team, are you our Michael Jordan or Latrell Sprewell?" He was a smart guy and caught on quick. As we continued our discussion, we made a list of his positive and negative contributions to our culture and talked about the effect on the team around him. I shared some feedback from a few exit interviews with new hires who decided to leave and mentioned him personally. Their thoughts were that if a top performer making a very high income spoke this way about working here, then the job was not worth investing the time. New hires were benchmarking our organization as a place to work factoring in his behavior.

The good news is we agreed to work together to make things better. I agreed to hear and address any concerns delivered in a professional manner, and he agreed to no more outbursts. It did not happen overnight and took time to change this behavior. Anytime he threw a tantrum, I would call him Latrell to remind him of the need to change. As time passed, he changed, and because issues were discussed in a more clinical manner, we worked together to improve. The residual benefit in addressing concerns helped all colleagues. His productivity as a top performer took center stage, and his input was making the team around him better. Our relationship also improved. When I was promoted to RVP and building our practice, I sent staff to his office for mentorship and invited him to my region to do training.

Like it or not, top producers set the example for the rest of the team. New colleagues will look to them as a sign of what the culture is more so than the leaders. What is even more important is, it will show the team the limits of acceptable or desired behavior. Michael Jordan is loved because he set an example of success based on hard work and conduct, on as well as off the court. Because of his professional approach, his results take center stage and elevate the play of the other players. Your top producers need to be like Mike. Give them a shot to turn things around as you roll out WeCulture. If you have a Latrell Sprewell, most will come around, provided you have the discipline to uphold the core values of WeCulture. If not, term them. In the short run, you will miss the production, but in the long run, you will keep countless new hires because of a healthy culture with core values governing behavior followed by all. Good culture breeds top producers; no one wants to replicate their version of Latrell.

As your organization adopts WeCulture, employees can reinforce core values through peer accountability. Every employee should be empowered to remind another when actions go against the company's stated core values and tenets. As stated earlier, our teams had WeCulture Fatheads on the office walls. At times while we were driving the change early on, I would joke with a colleague who fell off the wagon, "Come on, don't make me tap the sign. If we do that, is it really what WeCulture is all about?" What I was really saying was, "Is what we are doing or proposing truly reflecting our core values?" As WeCulture took hold, in interviews we would ask situational questions to see if potential hires shared these core values. If you are going to devote fifty-plus hours a week to a workplace, you should do everything you can to make it a great place to work. Colleagues can drive culture at the staff level with great effect. Govern your own behavior and hold your peers accountable. Sometimes this will be hard or may weed out a weak employee, but if you are with an organization for the long haul, it will contribute to making your job a place where you want to be.

WECULTURE FOR LEADERSHIP

The reality is no new initiative can succeed without 100 percent commitment from leaders, and WeCulture is no different. This is not because these individuals are in positions of power or influence; it is because they are on display to the team they are charged to lead. Managers are watched less by their boss and more by colleagues at the staff level. One of the top reasons people leave any organization is usually related to the relationship they have with their direct supervisors. Think about interactions with your colleagues each day and keep a journal for a few weeks. As you interact with your team, log the topics discussed, messages you were delivering, and the reaction of the people receiving the message. What is the pattern? Does your audience walk away with a clear message, a sense of purpose, and energy? Are expectations clear? We could offer hundreds of tips for leadership, and many books have already been written. Many are peppered through this book based on specific situations. I believe the best way to impact change is by first meeting the expectations of those you are charged.

In the book *The Truth About Leadership* by James Kouzes and Barry Posner, the authors conducted years of research on the expectations people have of leaders. The finding concluded that regardless of nationality, age, race, or industry, there are four top characteristics that people look for in their leaders.

More importantly the research was repeated and done over several years, proving that these traits are timeless. Part of WeCulture is that as we hire individuals to the organization, the team must evaluate if what we have to offer can meet the candidate's expectations. After we hire, how we engage our employees and leverage core values helps us shape desired behavior to create culture. To be an effective leader, we need to understand what our colleagues expect of us at the most fundamental level. Let's have a look at the top four characteristics, digging beyond the usual rhetoric and showmanship that makes so many leaders fail.

HONESTY

This characteristic tops the list and is also one of WeCulture's three core values. Trust is built on a foundation of setting a marker for doing what you say you will do. The definition from the dictionary: free from deceit, truthful and sincere in meaning. It is easy to understand why this was the top trait for leadership in the studies done, regardless of where or when the surveys were conducted. Let's set aside managing and leading for a moment; no relationship at a peer level can be successful without trust. If you are charged to lead, you are on display for everyone to see, and your colleagues will pay close attention to what you say and how it compares to what you actually do. Even momentary deviations from what you say you will do versus actions taken will immediately erode trust. Why? Because your actions are on display to a broader audience and setting the example. People will walk away interpreting the message and then compare it to action in their own ways. Most importantly the study done shows the need for honesty and that its impact on leadership will never change.

Social media has created forums of communication where anyone can share opinions and pass judgement. People now have the ability to share thoughts and opinions instantly to a broad audience with little to no restrictions imposed. If you are committed to WeCulture, then set the tone with your own behavior. In chapters three through five, we talked about Pedal the Bike, Be Positive, and Honest and Ethical. Nothing erodes morale more than a double standard for leadership. To avoid misunderstandings, transparency is key. If there is a change needed from what was a stated objective, sit down with your team and share what is happening and why. If you surround yourself with the right people who share your core values and core qualities, they will appreciate open discussion and support a needed change. Many times leaders will change direction and act without discussing why with their teams, leaving questions as to why unanswered. When this happens, your colleagues will be left alone with their thoughts to form their own opinions on why actions may not match words. Leaders who fail to communicate rarely get the benefit of a doubt.

A good example is when an employee leaves the company, regardless of voluntary or involuntary reasons. When I worked for publicly traded companies, when we terminated a colleague's employment, we would do it with coaching from human resources. Performance termination is usually pretty straightforward, with supporting documentation based on productivity tracked by KPI's. If you are practicing WeCulture's approach to Pedal the Bike, this information is public for all colleagues to see. Regardless I always expected direct supervisors to sit with colleagues and share the data, including the reason why the employee was no longer with the company. The challenge comes when we have an employee who is termed for a nonperformance reason: rules violation, harassment, discriminatory conduct, or, if you are committed to WeCulture, the employee did not reflect the core values through their actions. Because our society is so litigious in nature, as a manager, I was often coached not to share the reason we terminated an employee or to be vague to avoid legal risk. I learned the hard way; if we don't share the information, colleagues will form their own opinions of our actions, and often the terminated employee would fill in the blanks. Stop listening to your lawyers, and start trusting your employees and share the truth. If someone violates the rules of conduct or goes against core values, the team will appreciate leadership taking appropriate corrective action. Transparency builds trust.

FORWARD-LOOKING

Ranked second on the list is a leader's ability to be forward looking. With the demands of never-ending internal meetings, clients, and day-to-day workload, it is easy for even the most effective leader to become bogged down managing in the moment. The time goes by quickly, and before you know it, the team is off track. Being forward-looking means having a concern for the future of the team or organization. A key motivator for any employee is to be part of something for the greater good. A clear vision for the future can help display how routine, day-to-day tasks get us closer to achieving goals. Call it what you want, the message is simple: Leaders are expected to take action with a "destination" in mind. The best way to get buy-in is to state the mission and be transparent on the when, how, and why. Once people understand the reasons why behind the mission, we can then lay out the how, which is the path to get there. The daily grind of what needs to be done then becomes a means to our common end.

The best approach is to budget time for strategic planning. Sometimes the best way to lead is to be away from your team to take an objective look at the business. Once you have a good idea of where you are based on data and some well-needed self-reflection, you can re-engage the team and involve them in planning. So many managers pride themselves on how packed their calendars are with meetings, conference calls, and other recurring tactical appointments. The shroud of a busy day makes us feel effective, but the truth is we can easily lose sight of our strategic goals stuck at the task level. The best leaders have free time and are comfortable being alone to think. A residual effect will be time to recharge as well as regroup.

While establishing WeCulture in the first office location, this became the fuel for change. When I joined, this was one of the worst organizations in the company. We had no successful colleagues and no hope of achieving the financial goals set by the company. Our stated goal was to become a Circle of Excellence office and to have our colleagues make more money than last year. I started in April and finished the year ahead of expectations. The first full calendar year, the team achieved 50-percent top-line revenue growth, and our existing colleagues saw an increase on average of 40 percent in income from the prior year. While we were all focused on driving sales and placements each month, we met as a team and reviewed performance versus the stated goals to show progress. Before each meeting, I would take a long walk or lunch alone just to really think through where we were. Each week we had colleague one-on-one to review individual performance versus personal goals. On the first Monday of Q4, we met as a team and set a list of goals to plan for the next calendar year. Hearing the feedback, sharing the strategy, and executing with the team all set the stage for forward-thinking leadership, as well as forward-thinking teamwork.

INSPIRING

The definition of inspire: fill with the urge or ability to do or feel something. Leaders need to share genuine enthusiasm, excitement, and energy to motivate others to act. WeCulture's core value of Be Positive is born from this and a reminder to leaders and colleagues that how we approach the workplace will have a lasting impact on our abilities to be successful. We cannot expect our teams to give it their best without you setting the tone with your energy. A leader's optimism is a signal to the rest of the team that the strategic goals are indeed achievable. Once this vision is set, the team will be in the proper mindset to put in the work needed at the tactical level. The work we do today takes us one step closer to a better tomorrow.

One of the most famous men in American history is Dr. Martin Luther King. An American civil rights activist, Dr. King was a leader for advancing the rights of African Americans through nonviolent protests. His vision for the future had a defining moment in August 1963 during the March on Washington for Jobs and Freedom. His speech "I Have Dream" defined the goals of the civil rights movement and is ranked as one of the top speeches of the twentieth century. His dream was a land of equality born out of the legacy of slavery in America. The first step to this dream became reality when Congress passed the Civil Rights Act of 1968, known as the Fair Housing Act. This legislation paved the way for the future to prevent discrimination based on race, religion, national origin, sex, family status, or disability. His undying energy, unwavering vision, and commitment to the cause inspired a nation to change, improving the lives of millions of its own citizens. Change begins with a dream or vision; make your personal energy the spark to make the dream a reality.

COMPETENT

Competence is defined as the ability to do something successfully or efficiently. When looking at someone to lead, credibility will be built quickly on a track record of success or past execution. People often will assess the choice of following a leader based on past performance. The team will follow you if they are confident you know what you are doing. It lends credibility to what you say you will do because people can believe you have the skill and ability to follow through. In most cases, desire to achieve is not enough; skills and abilities will absolutely impact the end result. Knowledge and competence feeds personal confidence and will inspire others to execute. While this is critical for successful leaders, this does not imply that first-time leaders are doomed to failure or should not be trusted to lead. It means that a leader must have established experience that demonstrates knowledge to help us achieve our goals — maybe a top performer as an individual contributor, someone known from a competitor, or a colleague who has a reputation for working well on teams for special projects.

People who are competent also have the self-confidence to admit they don't know something but have the capability to learn. One myth worth addressing: Experience does not equal competence. Many people have experiences but, because of their own mindset or capacity, did not walk away with the lesson to apply in the future. Think of it this way: If I told you I had opened and launched five businesses in staffing, does this establish that competence? No, competence is completely dependent on the track record associated with it. If all five businesses failed and closed, then I have not displayed the competence to launch a business even though I experienced opening a business five times. If I opened one staffing company that was a success, sold for a profit, and is still thriving today, that experience now has a basis of competence attached to a track record of past success.

Competence is usually tied to effort. We have already talked about the book *Grit* by Angela Duckworth, and the general rule is achievement is a function of effort applied by a talented person to learn a skill. Effort is then applied to execute that skill to achieve the desired result. While in rare cases incompetence is not the fault of the individual, in business my observations show that incompetence is usually tied back to a lack of effort. This could be lack of effort in the thick of tactical execution or lack of effort during strategic planning to do the needed research. Either way, in the business world, it is proven time and time again that those who apply effort can excel regardless of circumstances. Sales is a forum to compete that is a grand equalizer. Leading teams I have seen people in obscure markets outperform others in the largest metropolis. In my first role as an RVP, I moved from the Northeast to a small region in what was considered a tier-three market. Our growth put us ranked fifth overall in the company, and we were one of the most profitable regions in the U.S. within a year. The people I was charged to lead were not remarkable in any way; they just executed and applied effort to what we taught them.

While these characteristics set the stage for leadership acceptance, nothing can outweigh your commitment through action. Strong leaders use the never-ending spotlight to display their commitment to core values through their own efforts. The spotlight of leadership can only yield two possible outcomes and exposes you for who you really are. The first is that you are the leader you claim to be governing your actions based on the core values of WeCulture — thus living up to the billing of the desired characteristics expected from those who choose to follow. The second outcome is that this spotlight burns, and being on constant display will expose you as a fraud. If you're someone who enjoys the little bit of power you have a little too much or the person that won't make the effort, or someone who says one thing and does another, then WeCulture becomes lip service. Be an example of what you expect and use the spotlight to showcase desired behavior.

EGO IS YOUR ENEMY

While you focus on leveraging WeCulture to drive results, keep this in mind: Your ego is the enemy. Ego is defined as a person's sense of self-esteem or self-importance; the higher you climb in success or leadership, the bigger it can get. If you are not aware, ego can be self-destructive, and if you are leading, there will be collateral damage. Here the saying, "We make our own monsters," proves to be true. Our ego is something we need to keep in check, and a critical part of WeCulture is taking responsibility for your own actions. There are a couple of common ego traps we unconsciously set for ourselves that are worth mentioning. Even if you are aware, there is no guarantee you will avoid them.

Don't fall in love with your successes. Even the greatest leaders can start off with the best intentions and be corrupted by achievements. As the leader wins, he or she slowly forgets that it was a team effort —the success counted on the support of others. A good sign this is happening is when you actually tell yourself that the team can't win without you. It is the first step away from effective leadership to becoming a self-important jerk. Our self-image is created in our own mind, so only you can prevent your ego from taking control. There are so many examples in the entertainment industry of common people making a meteoric rise to fame and fortune that allow their inflated sense of self to bring everything crashing down around them. Along with an inflated sense of self comes a false sense of invincibility; the result is reckless behavior as you abandon the core values that helped you win. Without core values to govern your behavior, your followers will eventually abandon you. We don't need to share a working example here. If you need one, reread chapter one — I know the trap well because I fell in it myself.

Our egos will drive decisions based on personal needs or pride over the greater good. I had a great boss early on in my career who gave me a piece of advice that helps me today. He told me, "In matters of business, your personal pride has no place." Your sense of self-image can often cloud your judgement. If you are always concerned about what others think in the short run of you personally, then it will be the primary driver in your decision-making process. Being a good leader requires that you act for the greater good of the team. You cannot lead without the ability to swallow your own personal pride or sacrifice your image. These are first-order consequences, meaning how things look in the moment. If you act based on how things look and put this before the longer-term goal, the team will suffer. Politicians deal with this because every word they say is scrutinized by the omnipresent media. Every interaction must be measured against how a news organization might spin it. Politicians often put first-order consequences over the long-term greater good to avoid controversy created by the media.

A final thought that will help: Leverage trust to forge relationships. I have worked for leaders who would tell me, "New hires have to earn trust," or to be mindful of how much trust I offered to the colleagues I was charged to lead. I look at this differently; in business I offer my trust immediately. I assume we are all working together and expect that people will do what they say they do until they don't. Think about new hires: Why do they have to earn trust? We spend time and money as an organization carefully executing our hiring process to find someone we believe to be the right person. Why on earth would we hire someone we did not trust? If we hired the right person, how does giving trust first help build great culture? If I meet someone in business, I offer trust immediately. Once I extend this other person trust, I can quickly figure out if they are actually trustworthy based on how they respond. As the right people are given trust, they will quickly reciprocate trust in return. This is a solid foundation to build lasting relationships. In the book *Speed of Trust* by Stephen Covey, a main point made is that business will pay a "tax" in time, money, and effort if colleagues don't trust each other. The tax is paid because people spend more time focused on motives, personal agendas, or just working against others, pulling effort away from the common goals to grow the business.

I did exit interviews with colleagues who left our teams in an effort to learn, and common feedback I would receive was that the colleague did not trust the manager. At first I really did not make the connection, but as I asked why, one former employee said he felt micromanaged and did not want to work for a manager he believed did not trust him. Because the leader did not offer trust first, this colleague could not offer trust in return. Without mutual trust, relationships are doomed to failure. Trust the people you work with each day; it can be a powerful tool to fuel cooperation. If people violate that trust, the good news is you will know who they really are quickly and can act accordingly.

We starts with you. The time we spend with our colleagues at work can be a place we look forward to each day or an unfulfilling hole that has a negative impact on the other parts of our lives. I know it sounds dramatic, but how satisfied we are at work directly impacts our lives outside of our jobs. Anything we devote so many hours to for the majority of our lifetimes deserves any effort to make it better. As you finish this book, ask yourself, "Who is going to work every day?" If you are a staff-level colleague, use WeCulture to govern your own actions and see if you can influence those around you. Be the spark and take ownership — WeCulture can and will start with you. As others feel the change and join you, we will include them too. Which brings me to final thoughts.

"To achieve anything, you need a burning desire."

— Napoleon Hill

CHAPTER TWELVE

BE WORTH IT

Most people expect companies to have a great culture. Unfortunately the vast majority do not and will need a spark for change. None of us are entitled to a job or career, much less a great place to work; we have to earn it every day. People create the fabric of what an organization's identity is; a company is only as good as the people it hires. As an owner of a small business, you cannot expect to grow through sheer force of will; the ability to scale your vision beyond your personal reach will be what makes the difference. The name on the front door has no life without the actions of people who work behind it. If you want your job, team, or company to be great — a place you look forward to going to each day, something you are proud to be a part of — you need to be worth it. We established in chapter two of this book that all colleagues at all levels create the culture of an organization. If we as employees have the expectation for the place we work to give us great opportunities, we need to accept our share of that responsibility. "Be Worth It" is my own personal motto, and I would like to share what it means from the perspective of leadership and for staff colleagues.

Leadership is a gift earned through deeds that makes you a servant to those who follow you. Just because you have a title and individuals reporting to you, this does not make you a leader. This does not make the people reporting to you a team. Your title manager, RVP, CEO, CFO, CIO, regardless of what it is, only guarantees you are the one responsible for those you are charge to lead. It makes you accountable for achieving the collective goals and productivity and to ensure delivery of whatever work product the group is responsible for. Maybe you are a sales manager — ultimately your title only guarantees you are responsible for the results of the people reporting to you. If you are a plant manager, your title makes you responsible for running a safe, efficient, and productive operation, achieving manufacturing goals. In both cases, this does not guarantee people will follow you. You have to show through your actions that you are worth it.

As discussed in chapter eleven, leadership is based on honesty, vision for the future, the ability to inspire, and competence. All of these leadership qualities require hard work and dedication to the greater good from the person charged to lead. Don't look at your team as people required to follow; my approach is to be worth their loyalty. A great way to do this is to remind yourself that the leader is the servant to those who follow. WeCulture's mission is to focus on employee engagement by embracing core values to grow the business. People want to believe in what they are doing and be a part of something bigger than the jobs at their desks. Being in staffing for almost twenty years, I have heard from almost every person I ever helped find a job, "I want to find a long-term home." What does this mean? People don't want to change jobs unless they have to. Changing jobs is stressful and, in reality, a controlled risk. If people want to find a home, this creates an opportunity for those in charge to lead. If people have an inherent desire to stay with a good company, then to retain a great team, all we have to do is create a great work environment. WeCulture creates core values that must be followed by all with the goal in mind to create that great place to work. Once our colleagues believe they have found a home, we can retain our best talent to achieve our financial goals. We create loyalty through trust. We inspire our teams by connecting them to a common vision. We share the vision of how the work we do today builds for tomorrow. We show our own commitment to the team through personal actions. As we achieve results together, leaders win the confidence of their teams and the loyalty of their colleagues. When you have the right people working together, WeCulture will help accomplish the goal of every business — to make money. Even if you are in a nonprofit, you are working to make money for a cause. You can only get so far alone; if you want to create a following, then you have to show people you can be worth it.

Some managers count on fear as a motivator, and in the short term, this might work, but this does not build a loyal following. There are many leaders who still believe they can drive results by reminding staff of consequences. I have been to "all-hands" staff meetings on more than one occasion where executives have told teams that if results don't improve, they will make changes. I watched a COO of a publicly traded company completely lose his sense of self-control on a call with RVPs and managing directors, threatening jobs and swearing. The impact to morale and productivity was long-lasting, and his moment of weakness of placing blame on his subordinates broke the trust. After the call, a few resignations followed, but what he did not see were the hours wasted as his team focused on his behavior without hearing what was actually said. Some of the managers actually projected this behavior down to their colleagues — maybe because they did not know better or they could not hide the stress. The reality is your best people don't have to tolerate bad leadership. The market creates too many opportunities for talented colleagues. Use fear, and any short-term gain will have the long-term price of resignations from your best people. Without a talented group of followers, you will not get far.

For colleagues be worth it has a different meaning. Think about it. You spend the majority of your waking hours at your job if you work full-time. In today's job market, you probably went through a long, arduous interview process where you were tested and questioned seemingly without end. You likely had to compete with other applicants to win the job. What is most important to remember is that when the offer was made to join the organization, you made the choice to accept it. If you are going to go through all this time and trouble to be part of an organization and if you made the personal choice to join the team, you owe it to yourself and your colleagues to make the most of it. Be worth it.

If you work in a toxic environment, before you quit, take a chance and be the spark. Change all starts with the first action, and little things matter. Simple things can help lift your mood and the people around you. Greeting colleagues with a smile, taking a walk on a nice day during a scheduled break, helping a peer that might be struggling a bit, or taking time to make a new colleague feel welcome are a few easy ways to start. Adopt WeCulture core values on your own and see if it rubs off on the people around you. We all can control our own behavior and leverage it to shape the workplace around us. Put your best effort in every day; Pedal the Bike to help your team. If faced with a challenge, focus on the solution and everyone's part to get there; Be Positive. Say "we can" every time someone else says "we can't." Hold yourself to a high standard and be Honest and Ethical in your actions, even if those around you do not and even if it means some personal sacrifice. You don't need a title or assigned followers from the company to lead others. Actions are what will inspire the people around you. If you succeed, then you will not only be a part of something great, but you were part of what made it great. If you fail, then you know you gave it everything you had and can feel confident in a choice to move on.

There were many people who helped me make WeCulture a reality. While the concept is something I created, the idea was only a spark — I was only one person, hardly "we." It was born as I learned through a very personal failure. I ask you, the reader, the question I asked myself as I created WeCulture: If you are aware of the challenge, then what are you prepared to do to make the change? You can put this book down and agree or disagree with the concept of WeCulture, but the reality is the world of work has changed, and how we engage our employees will determine the results for any organization. Defined core values can govern behavior and give colleagues common focus. Get the team working toward a common goal — a greater good — and they will be loyal to your organization. Retain your best people — now you are not alone. You have the help you need to push the dream farther and expand your vision through the ability to scale the business. WeCulture helps establish the core values to govern behavior supporting the ability to build bigger. As a business owner, you don't need to touch everything if you have actively engaged employees who share your core values. The core values and tenets for your company will guide choices and decisions made by the new leaders you develop to help you grow the business. There is no limit to what can be achieved for effective leaders. There is nothing preventing anyone from being a leader, nothing stopping you from changing your own behavior to lead by example.

As the old guard of Baby Boomers retires, taking their experience, skills, knowledge, and work ethic with them, it can leave businesses that do not change vulnerable. As Millennials become the majority of the workforce, they bring different expectations of their employers, and they also bring different skills. To get access to the best and brightest, how we attract talent needs to change. To unlock the full potential of the next generation, work environments must adapt and create a focus on teams over individual achievement. Think of the edge your business would have if you were able to actively engage employees to drive results, if your employees were part of the 33 percent minority of people who enjoy their jobs. How would it impact results? Customer satisfaction? Productivity? What edge would that give you over the other teams that are part of the 66 percent majority of people not satisfied and disengaged from their work? Richard Branson, founder of Virgin, believes the success of his organization is built on the effort of the employees who follow him. One of my favorite quotes is, "Clients do not come first; employees come first. If you take care of your employees, they will take care of your clients."

Take time to reflect for the next thirty days. Do you look forward to going to work the majority of the time? As you talk to your colleagues, are they part of the 33 percent of actively engaged people or part of the 66 percent of our workforce that is disengaged or dissatisfied with their work? How does this impact the business? Your personal income? Your life outside of work? After careful thought, if you believe things need to change, it is time for the hard question: What are you prepared to do? Every day you let pass not realizing your full potential is time you cannot get back. Look at the opportunity you have and make a commitment to give it your best and be worth it. Let WeCulture guide you to include your employees, peers, and leaders too.

CPSIA information can be obtained
at www.ICGtesting.com
Printed in the USA
LVHW041749150519
617950LV00017B/998